MOT ET PARTIES DU DISCOURS
WORD AND WORD CLASSES
WORT UND WORTARTEN

LA PENSÉE LINGUISTIQUE

Collection dirigée

par

P. SWIGGERS et W. VAN HOECKE

VOLUME 1

MOT ET PARTIES DU DISCOURS
WORD AND WORD CLASSES
WORT UND WORTARTEN

sous la direction de

Pierre SWIGGERS et Willy VAN HOECKE

avec la collaboration de

André MARTINET
Robert H. ROBINS
Wolfgang P. SCHMID

PEETERS LEUVEN-PARIS

LEUVEN UNIVERSITY PRESS

ISBN 90-6831-055-0
D. 1986/0602/13

TABLE DES MATIÈRES

Avant-propos, *P. Swiggers* et *W. Van Hoecke* 7
The *Technē grammatikē* of Dionysius Thrax in its historical perspective: the evolution of the traditional European word class systems, *R.H. Robins* 9
Mot et partie du discours dans la grammaire française aux XVIIe et XVIIIe siècles, *P. Swiggers* 38
Que faire du «mot»?, *A. Martinet* 75
Eine revidierte Skizze einer allgemeinen Theorie der Wortarten, *W.P. Schmid* 85
Bibliographie sélective, *P. Swiggers* et *W. Van Hoecke* 100

AVANT-PROPOS

Ce recueil est consacré à un problème essentiel en linguistique générale: la définition du *mot* et son rapport (plus ou moins explicite) avec la théorie des *parties du discours*. Héritage d'une longue tradition européenne, ces notions, flottantes et généralement peu approfondies, ont pu fatiguer les esprits et décourager même les chercheurs les plus assidus: cela explique sans doute pourquoi elles sont couramment utilisées dans la plupart des théories linguistiques actuelles sans être définies. Il ne s'agira pas ici d'accuser les théoriciens de myopie ou de manque de sérieux; d'ailleurs, ni la notion de «mot», ni le système des parties du discours sont indispensables à l'élaboration d'une grammaire scientifique. Mais des difficultés surgissent là où de telles notions, historiquement chargées et très complexes, sont utilisées sans être définies (et souvent sans être situées dans une perspective diachronique). Pour cette raison, il a paru utile de retracer quelques grandes étapes dans le développement de la théorie des parties du discours: cette histoire est aussi celle du refoulement du mot, entité posée ou présupposée, mais toujours approchée par un biais oblique.

La partie *historique* (contributions de R.H. Robins et de P. Swiggers) montre que les définitions du mot dans la tradition grammaticale de l'Occident reposent toujours sur une classification des parties du discours. Depuis l'Antiquité, le mot a donc moins été défini en fonction de son statut descriptif que par rapport à l'établissement de classes dans lesquelles apparaissent des *types de mots*. Le système dégagé par les grammairiens antiques ne sera pas modifié par ceux du moyen âge: les grammairiens médiévaux acceptent les huit parties du discours reconnues par les grammairiens romains, tout en accordant une place prépondérante aux noms et aux verbes, dont la combinaison constitue une proposition. Le mérite principal des modistes consistera à expliquer le système des parties du discours en fonction de notre perception intellective du monde. C'est à l'époque de la Renaissance que les grammairiens (Ramus et Sanctius en particulier) redécouvrent la tripartition antique des mots en noms, verbes et «autres mots». Mais ce n'est qu'aux XVIIe et XVIIIe siècles qu'une perspective proprement syntaxique se fait jour dans la grammaire (française), et que la classification des mots fait l'objet d'une réflexion théorique, qui a conservé sa valeur.

Cette problématique liée des mots et des parties du discours (en tant que classes de mots) appelle une réflexion *systématique* (cf. les contributions d'A. Martinet et de W.P. Schmid) sur ces deux notions. Dans le cas du mot, celle-ci doit commencer par l'examen critique de la possibilité même de définir le mot. Un tel examen prend sa place dans une recherche épistémologique globale sur les fondements de la linguistique générale et sur les unités de description. Quant aux classes de mots, leur nombre et leur spécificité doivent être déterminés en fonction d'un système de propriétés (phonologiques, morphologiques, syntaxiques, sémantico-pragmatiques...), et il incombe au linguiste de justifier ce système.

Le but de ce volume n'est pas de dire le dernier mot sur le *mot*; au contraire, il devrait stimuler l'intérêt que portent linguistes, philosophes et psychologues à des notions linguistiques, que d'aucuns considèrent comme évidentes, et d'autres comme incertaines, spéculatives et partant comme contestables. Nous espérons que le contenu de ce volume sera suffisamment riche pour stimuler la réflexion critique des lecteurs intéressés[1].

P. SWIGGERS - W. VAN HOECKE

[1] Nous tenons à remercier nos collaborateurs étrangers, MM. A. Martinet, R.H. Robins et W.P. Schmid, pour leur contribution fort appréciée. Nos remerciements vont également à la Commission des Publications de la K.U.Leuven et en particulier à son président, M.F. Neirynck, dont l'aide financière et l'appui moral ont rendu possible la publication de ce volume. Nous n'oublions pas Mmes M. Goyens et H. Hermans, qui ont collaboré à la réalisation matérielle de ce volume avec dévouement et efficacité.

R.H. ROBINS
(School of Oriental and African Studies; University of London)

THE *TECHNĒ GRAMMATIKĒ* OF DIONYSIUS THRAX IN ITS HISTORICAL PERSPECTIVE: THE EVOLUTION OF THE TRADITIONAL EUROPEAN WORD CLASS SYSTEMS*

Dionysius Thrax was for many centuries considered to have been the first author of a very short and concise grammar of classical Greek, the first extant grammar of Greek to be written, and the first extant grammar of any language written in the western world. The whole work, which was known as τέχνη γραμματική (grammar) and may have been referred to also as τὰ παραγγέλματα (instructions), comprises no more than fifteen pages of text as printed in Bekker's edition (1816) and is divided into twenty-five sections. The text is followed by 326 pages of scholia or notes by various later writers, giving some indication of the interest aroused by the work in classical and Byzantine times. The value of the scholia is very uneven, but many useful and pertinent comments and explanations are included in them[1].

Questions about the authenticity of the text as we have it have been raised since antiquity (see Bekker 1816: 672-673), and its authorship has been discussed by several scholars since the beginning of the nineteenth century. Generally the bulk of the text has been accepted as the work of Dionysius (cp. Lersch 1840; Schmidt 1852-1853; Steinthal 1890-1891[2]; Pauly - Wissowa 1893-1972, s.v. Dionysios Thrax; Traglia 1956), but a more serious challenge was raised by di Benedetto (1958-1959) in the light of certain grammatical writings preserved in papyri. The whole question is summarized by Pinborg (1975: 103-106), who broadly agrees with di Benedetto that the sections following section one (Bekker 1816:

* This article is based on a revision and integration of two previously published papers: «Dionysius Thrax and the western grammatical tradition» (*Transactions of the Philological Society* 1957. 67-106), and «The development of the word class system of the European grammatical tradition» (*Foundations of Language* 2. 3-19, 1966). I am indebted to the editors and publishers of these periodicals for their permission to reuse parts of the material published therein.

[1] Text of the *Technē* in Bekker (1816: 627-643). The comments of the scholiasts appear on pages 645-972. A later edition of the text is to be found in Uhlig (1883) and Pecorella (1962).

629 § 1) are from a later grammar, perhaps of the third or fourth century A.D., tacked on to the introduction to a lost work by Dionysius. The date and the genuineness of the first section as belonging to around 100 B.C. are supported by direct quotations naming Dionysius in Sextus Empiricus's *Adversus grammaticos* 57, 72, 250 and by the definition of grammar given by Varro (first century B.C.; Funaioli 1907: 265): «Ars grammatica scientia est eorum quae a poetis historicis oratoribusque dicuntur ex parte maiore», which looks like a close adaptation of the definition given in the *Technē*: «γραμματική ἐστιν ἐμπειρία τῶν παρὰ ποιηταῖς τε καὶ συγγραφεῦσιν ὡς ἐπὶ τὸ πολὺ λεγομένων».

Since Pinborg's 1975 survey an important further study of the available grammatical papyri has been undertaken by Wouters (1979; see also 1976). Wouters gives the texts of sixteen papyri from Egypt purporting to be *technai grammatikai*, which were written at periods between the first and the sixth centuries A.D., together with some commentaries on specific linguistic topics such as participles, prosodies and the Greek past tense augment. The papyri are fragmentary, though Wouters has restored as much of the text as is possible. But it is now clear that the form and the content of the *Technē* as we now have it were followed by the writers of these later grammars. As Wouters says (1979: 41): «On the whole the manuals in the papyri have the same structure as Dionysius' work». Most significantly, the first text in the collection, dated around 9-12 A.D., copies (Wouters 1979: 49) the definition of λόγος, sentence, from section 13 of the *Technē* (Bekker 1816: 634). In the light of this latest papyrological evidence Wouters concludes (1979: 36), as did Pecorella (1962), that the *Technē* is substantially the work of Dionysius Thrax, though he adds that in view of its popularity and its regular use as a textbook it must have undergone various textual changes over the centuries.

This question of authorship is clearly an important one in classical philology. It is rather less crucial in the history of linguistics. A grammar of Greek by Dionysius was available in the first century B.C. (Pauly - Wissowa 1893-1972: s.v. Dionysios Thrax, 980), and it would appear that this set out a description of Greek phonetics and morphology substantially as this is set out in the text that we have. The eight word class system, which a scholiast said was one of Dionysius's major contributions (Bekker 1816: 676, 724) and which may go back to his teacher Aristarchus (Lersch 1840: 59-64), was the framework used and taken for granted by Apollonius Dyscolus (c. 200 A.D.), assuming essentially the same definitions and employing the same categories as those established by the writer of the *Technē*. With these considerations in mind no harm is done by continuing to refer to the text of the *Technē* that we have as the grammar of Dionysius Thrax.

The debt of current grammars of Greek to Dionysius's work, which remained a standard Greek grammar for thirteen centuries (Sandys 1920: 139), would be hard to overestimate, and in a more general context it has been said that «there is scarcely a textbook on English grammar that does not display evidence of its debt to Dionysius Thrax» (Forbes 1933: 112). The grammatical scholarship of Alexandria and elsewhere in the Greek world, of which the *Technē* is one of the exponents, is a significant part of the culture of antiquity. The *Technē* is clearly the result of a long tradition of linguistic studies extending over several generations (from the Pre-Socratics, in fact) of which it represents the culmination (Traglia 1956: 38).

Of the life and personality of Dionysius little is known. He lived during the latter part of the second century B.C. and during the early years of the first. He was a member of the well-known Alexandrian group of literary scholars working under the patronage of the Ptolemies. He was a pupil of the great Homeric scholar Aristarchus, and he was a Homeric scholar himself; we are told that in the course of his teaching while he was in Rhodes he manufactured a model of Nestor's drinking cup from its description in the *Iliad* (XI, lines 632-635), the necessary silver being contributed by his students (Athenaeus XI, 480a).

Alexandrian scholarship was a part, and perhaps the main part, of the intellectual life of the Hellenistic age[2]. This period of Greek history, which may be roughly said to have begun in the second half of the fourth century B.C., was marked politically by the break-up of the city-states as separate and independent civic entities and by the spread and development of a generalized Greek culture, with various non-Greek admixtures, over the greater part of the Greek world of the time. All this found its reflex in literary and linguistic studies; educated Greek speakers became conscious of the growing discrepancy between current *Umgangssprachen* and the patterns of earlier Attic Greek, and with this went the quest for Ἑλληνισμός, defined as κατωρθωμενὴ λέξις, correct speech, free of barbarisms and non-Attic dialect features. In literature the classical authors were looked back to as models of a golden age of

[2] The bibliography on this period of history is extensive. Attention may be drawn to Susemihl (1891-1892), Sandys (1920[3]: 103-166), Bury (1923), and more recently Pfeiffer (1968: part 2), but in regard to the history of linguistics in Hellenistic times the account given in Steinthal (1890-1891[2]: vol. II, 1-68) remains most valuable.

the Greek language, and in Homeric scholarship research was devoted to the establishment of correct and uncorrupted texts of the *Iliad* and the *Odyssey*. These were two of the factors stimulating and guiding the growth of linguistic scholarship, part of the scholarship carefully fostered by the Macedonian courts then in control of the Greek world.

Grammar and linguistic studies in general served the needs of the critical commentary and the elucidation of classical texts. In this connection one may note the change in meaning of the word φιλόλογος in the course of years. For Plato the word designated an educated person, one given to the cultured use of language and in particular to philosophical discourse. In Hellenistic times the word began to refer rather to a student or a teacher of literature and of correct standards enshrined therein, thus somewhat resembling the continental European use of *Philologie* and similar words today[3].

The Hellenistic age was characterized by a greater separation and mutual independence among the various branches of learning, and grammar was acquiring a more self-contained status as a scholarly pursuit, though within the purview of literary studies; but it should be borne in mind that it had its own history.

For the pioneers of Greek grammar Greek was an unanalysed language. It is hard today not to envisage Greek set out in the way it has come to be set out, largely on the basis of the summary description in the *Technē*, and one is tempted to look on the work of Aristotle and the Stoics, the two main exponents of grammar before the Alexandrians, as the progressive discovery or revelation of an already existent set of classes and categories. Certainly Greek (like Latin) was predisposed towards the sort of grammar imposed on it in a way that other languages to which the system has been unimaginatively applied were not. In this sense the Greek grammarians succeeded because Greek was «like that». But we can hardly say that this was the only grammatical model available or that the system of eight word classes and the categories associated with them were the only satisfactory ones. It may have been the best system, and certainly the subsequent modifications have been in the form of rearrangements within an accepted frame. But prior to the establishment of this system we cannot say that different procedures might not have been followed.

One must recall the philosophical background to all Greek thinking about language. The first structural division of the Greek sentence was

[3] See further Steinthal (1890-1891[2]: vol. II, 14-16); Liddell - Scott (1940[9]: s.v. φιλόλογος).

made in terms of subject and predicate (ὄνομα and ῥῆμα) by Plato (*Sophistēs*), and this first dichotomy was developed on more strictly morphological lines to grow into the noun — verb distinction, later to develop by stages into the eight parts of speech or word classes recognized by the Alexandrians. While in Hellenistic times grammar tended to be regarded as part of the study of literature rather than of philosophy, philosophical considerations were always relevant, and the development of grammatical theory and method was influenced all the time by the most noteworthy controversy on language in antiquity, that of Analogy versus Anomaly, each championed by rival schools of philosophy (Steinthal 1890-1891[2]: vol. II, 71-161; Colson 1919).

The two themes had their defenders in two centres of Hellenistic learning, Alexandria and Pergamum, and this was a feature of the rivalry between these two schools. One can sympathize with Classen's dismissal of the whole controversy as quite unimportant (1829: 80 «Tota ista disceptatio vix tanto hiatu digna esse videtur»), framed as it was in terms that would hardly be used as they stand today. It is, however, important in any study of grammatical scholarship in antiquity as part of the context within which linguistic thought was promoted and developed.

The analogists insisted on the inherent orderliness and regularity of language, particularly in its grammatical aspect, and they undertook to show that grammatically comparable words exhibited similar inflectional paradigms and similar patterns of accentuation, and that grammatical categories were in the main congruent with the semantic categories of the denotata of the words concerned. The anomalists stressed the opposite thesis, that language is far from orderly, and that the rules and regularities sought by the analogists were shot through with exceptions. Aristarchus, the teacher of Dionysius, was regarded in antiquity as the champion of analogy, while Crates of Pergamum strenuously maintained the anomalist position (Gellius, *Noctes atticae* II: 25).

Varro (*De lingua latina*, Books VIII and IX) remains our main source for the details of this long-lasting controversy. Having read the Greek writers on it he applied their arguments to Latin. A trace of the sort of argumentation involved may be preserved in Book VIII: 68-69: the anomalists' challenge to a rule (*analogia*) by reference to apparent exceptions to it is met by a more careful restatement of the rule (Robins 1976).

It may be observed that the analogists, who insisted on the very conditions that make a scientific study of language possible, were mainly of the Alexandrian school and primarily interested in the study of language as part of the study of literature, whereas the anomalists were for the most part inspired by Stoic philosophy and concerned with language as part of a wider investigation of human thought[4]. The anomalists found no lack of examples that seemed to support their case against the regularities and correspondences adduced by the analogists: «anomalous» plural forms for single entities (Θῆβαι, Ἀθῆναι), words negative in form but with positive meaning (ἀθάνατος, deathless), the «anomaly» of masculine or feminine nouns with inanimate references, and the numerous exceptions and suppletions that must be recognized in the statement of almost any Greek verb paradigm. But the fact that these exceptions and irregular forms and relations were themselves noticeable could only have come about against a background of the more regular systems and associations established by the analogists. Two factors must be kept in mind in examining this controversy in antiquity: firstly the absence of any preexisting codified grammar of Greek (or of any other language available to the Greeks), with the regularities tabulated and set out in formal paradigms, and secondly the lack of a distinction among the Greek grammarians between inflectional and derivational formations, the latter being in most languages subject to less strict rules than the former (cp. Colson 1919: 26).

The analogist doctrine can be traced back at least as far as Aristotle, in whose writings ἀναλογία and kindred terms play a considerable part[5]. If analogy represents Aristotelianism in linguistic theory it is consonant with the Aristotelian view of language as conventional (θέσει) in essence (Allen 1948: 41-42; Collart 1954: 264); conventions that are orderly and systematic will more efficiently serve their purpose. Thus ἀναλογία is linked with θέσις and ἀνωμαλία with φύσις, two opposing terms in another early linguistic controversy (Steinthal 1890-1891²: vol. I, 319-374; Robins 1979²: 18-22). The Stoics asserted that language was a natural product; this was in harmony with their general emphasis on nature, φύσις, as the key to human life, but in part it also seems to have sprung from an excessive place assigned by them to onomatopoeia and sound symbolism in the formation of speech[6]. If

[4] Cp. Diogenes Laertius VII. 83: «πάντα γὰρ τὰ πράγματα διὰ τῆς ἐν λόγοις θεωρίας ὁρᾶσθαι, ὅσα τε τοῦ φυσικοῦ τόπου τυγχάνει καὶ αὖ πάλιν ὅσα τοῦ ἠθικοῦ».

[5] Cp. *Nicomachean ethics* 1131a 29: «ἔστιν ἄρα τὸ δίκαιον ἀνάλογόν τι»; 1131a 31: «ἡ γὰρ ἀναλογία ἰσότης ἐστι λόγων»; see also 1096b 28, 1106a 36, *Physics* 1. 7, 191a 8.

[6] Cp. Origen, *Against Celsus* 1. 24: «πότερον ὡς οἴεται Ἀριστοτέλης, θέσει εἰσὶ τὰ ὀνόματα, ἤ, ὡς νομίζουσιν οἱ ἀπὸ τῆς Στοᾶς, φύσει, μιμουμένων τῶν πρώτων φωνῶν τὰ πράγματα, καθ' ὧν τὰ ὀνόματα».

speech is natural rather than conventional in essence and in origin then it follows that its irregularities, disharmonies and «anomalies» are no less a proper part of language than the regularities and «analogies».

One can understand the lack of interest in the details of this controversy affected by Classen and by others in modern times. Neither side formulated their arguments in terms that would be used today, and many of their arguments seem either naively obvious or naively absurd. It is, however, fair to remember the pioneering nature of Greek linguistic speculation; we can hardly demand that they should have set about their problems and attempted their solutions in terms deemed appropriate today, after many centuries of linguistic scholarship.

It was against the background of this controversy that Alexandrian linguistic scholarship developed. Aristarchus, one of the founders of Homeric scholarship and of the scientific study of Greek (Sandys 1920: 131-136), used and expounded analogical principles in editing the Homeric texts and establishing correct readings in the manuscripts. Such work on the part of Aristarchus and others led to the systematic and detailed formulation of the ἀναλογίαι or regular grammatical patterns of the Greek language. It is fair to say that descriptive grammar in the west was developed through the working out of the principles of analogy, as this was understood by its adherents, on the Greek language of Homeric and other classical literature, and in the face of criticism from the sceptical anomalists. We notice that ἀναλογία, regularity, appears in Dionysius's definition of grammar as a field of study.

The *Technē* begins with an extensive definition of the subject of grammar, in which Dionysius also sets down what he considers to be the place of this subject in the wider field of education and scholarschip (§ 1):

«Grammar is the empirical knowledge of the general usages of poets and prose writers. It has six parts: first, accurate reading (aloud) with due regard for the prosodies; second, the explanation of the literary expressions in the works; third, the provision of notes on vocabulary and subject matter; fourth, the discovery of etymologies; fifth, the working out of regularities (ἀναλογίας ἐκλογισμός); sixth, the critical appreciation of literary compositions, which is the noblest part of the science»[7].

[7] «Γραμματική ἐστιν ἐμπειρία τῶν παρὰ ποιηταῖς τε καὶ συγγραφεῦσιν ὡς ἐπὶ τὸ πολὺ λεγομένων. Μέρη δὲ αὐτῆς εἰσὶν ἕξ· πρῶτον ἀνάγνωσις ἐντριβὴς κατὰ προσῳδίαν, δεύτερον ἐξήγησις κατὰ τοὺς ἐνυπάρχοντας ποιητικοὺς τρόπους, τρίτον γλωσσῶν τε καὶ ἱστοριῶν πρόχειρος ἀπόδοσις, τέταρτον ἐτυμολογίας εὕρεσις, πέμπτον ἀναλογίας ἐκλογισμός, ἕκτον κρίσις ποιημάτων, ὃ δὴ κάλλιστόν ἐστι πάντων τῶν ἐν τῇ τέχνῃ».

This introductory paragraph is important as being the first known attempt in Europe to define grammar (or linguistics in general) and to assign it a definite place within the world of learning. Grammatical studies had begun within the embrace of philosophy. The predominant influence of literary criticism and of the teaching of classical Greek was a feature of the Hellenistic age, and the Graeco-Roman papyri show that this was a continuing influence (Wouters 1979: 213). Dionysius's definition of grammar as essentially a propaedeutic to the study of literature became the standard one during succeeding centuries, being either assumed or repeated by the later grammarians, until the scholastic writers of the *grammaticae speculativae* in the later Middle Ages reorientated the subject fundamentally by bringing it back wholly under the control of an overall philosophical system.

Despite the wide-ranging list of topics falling within the purview of grammar as set out in the introductory paragraph, the *Technē* largely confines itself to what today would be designated as phonology and morphology. But a scholiast elaborates on the broader aspects of the subjects by explaining that, while dialectic, rhetoric, and grammar all deal with sentences,

> «the concern of dialectic is truth, that of rhetoric persuasiveness, but the grammarian is engaged on the comprehension of the sentence, what it means and how it expresses its meaning, for example, by what kinds of components the sentence is made manifest»[8].

The term γραμματική showed a change in its signification during antiquity similar to the change noticed earlier in the word φιλόλογος. Two different uses of γραμματική were noted by the scholiasts, who distinguished μικρά or παλαιά γραμματική (grammar in the restricted or earlier sense) from μεγάλη or νεωτέρα γραμματική (grammar in the wider or modern sense; Bekker 1816: 658, 667, 729). The former, which one commentator declared was older than the Trojan War, dealt only with reading aloud, writing, and the phonetic values of the letters; the latter had as its aim correct Greek (Ἑλληνισμός), a good written style, and the general study of literature. What seems to be an intermediate use of the word is mentioned by one scholiast (Bekker 1816: 736-737) who says that γραμματική was once divided into four parts, διορθωτικόν, ἀναγνωστικόν, ἐξηγητικόν, and κριτικόν. Three of these corres-

[8] Bekker (1816: 658): «τῆς μὲν γὰρ διαλεκτικῆς τἀληθές, τῆς δὲ ῥητορικῆς τὸ πείθειν, τῆς δὲ γραμματικῆς τέλος ἐστὶν ἡ κατάληψις τοῦ λόγου, τουτέστι τὸ διδάσκειν τί σημαίνει καὶ πῶς σημαίνει, οἷον διὰ ποίων μερῶν ὁ λόγος δηλοῦται.»

pond to the first, second, and last divisions of γραμματική as understood by Dionysius, and the scholiast explains that Dionysius's third, fourth, and fifth parts were the result of subdividing τὸ διορθωτικόν. Thus ἀναλογίας ἐκλογισμός, the part of γραμματική most nearly corresponding to *grammar* today, was expressly included in the comprehension of the word relatively late in its history, no doubt during and as part of the analogist-anomalist controversy.

The apparently simple definition of grammar as empirical knowledge, with which Dionysius opens his work, gave rise to a great outpouring of comments from the scholiasts, which must have reflected widespread protests at the implications of this definition. The use of the term ἐμπειρία, empirical knowledge, was resented as degrading the science of grammar. The context of this was the scale of intellectual activities referred to elsewhere (Bekker 1816: 656): πεῖρα, ἐμπειρία, τέχνη, ἐπιστήμη, which may be translated as «skill», «empirical knowledge», «science» and «understanding». 'Επιστήμη, the highest, was infallible by its nature, geometry and (in the culture of antiquity) astronomy being given as examples. Τέχνη was superior to ἐμπειρία by virtue of its operation in accordance with a realized methodological principle (λόγος; Bekker 1816: 664, 726-727). The distinction of τέχνη and ἐμπειρία by the former being principled (λόγον ἔχουσα) is familiar elsewhere in Greek thought[9].

This early criticism of Dionysius's definition may be seen as one of the first phases in a continuing division of opinion on the proper conception of linguistics that has continued through the history of the subject up to the present day, its most recent manifestation being the criticism by the Chomskyans of what they consider the «narrow empiricism» of the Bloomfieldian structuralists (cp. Chomsky 1964: 113; Robins 1974). Fairly recently Chomsky has insisted that the linguist should go beyond the mere statement of facts, «organizing linguistic data», to the uncovering of the «psychological reality» behind them if linguistics is to be truly scientific (1979: 119).

Dionysius's first subdivision of grammar, correct reading aloud, is described in the section following the definition. The subject matter is

[9] Bekker (1816: 732); cp. Plato, *Gorgias* 465a: «τέχνην δὲ αὐτὴν οὔ φημι εἶναι ἀλλ' ἐμπειρίαν, ὅτι οὐκ ἔχει λόγον οὐδένα ὧν προσφέρει, ὁποῖ' ἄττα τὴν φύσιν ἐστίν, ὥστε τὴν αἰτίαν ἑκάστου μὴ ἔχειν εἰπεῖν· ἐγὼ δὲ τέχνην οὐ καλῶ, ὃ ἂν ᾖ ἄλογον πρᾶγμα»; Aristotle, *Nicomachean ethics* 1142a 15-16: «πλῆθος γὰρ χρόνου ποιεῖ τὴν ἐμπειρίαν». This controversy goes back as far as Asclepiades (first century B.C., Sextus Empiricus, *Adversus grammaticos* 72).

envisaged as literature in its various forms, and he lists the different styles of reading appropriate to tragedy, comedy, elegy, and lyric poetry. The term προσῳδία is twice mentioned as an essential part of correct reading; though he does not say anything about it, in view of the current phonological use of the term *prosody* (Palmer 1970) it is interesting to see what the scholiasts have to say on this. The phonetic features covered by the word προσῳδία are the three pitch accents, length and shortness of vowels, and certain processes referred to as πάθη (modifications): elision of a final vowel before a word-initial vowel following without pause, what might be called close juncture (ὑφέν) and open juncture (ὑποδιαστολή). Ὑφέν designated the pronunciation of two words in close syntactic union as one phonological structure and also the unifying features of compound words. Ὑποδιαστολή referred to the phonetic features associated with word division, particularly where ambiguity might result from careless reading; an example given was ἔστιν ἄξιος «he is worthy», and ἔστι Νάξιος, «he is a Naxian». It appears that a distinctive pronunciation was available, with the syllabification of *n* with the preceding vowel in the first case and with the following vowel in the second; a facultative glottal stop after ἔστιν, as in the comparable English example *an ocean* (as against *a notion*), cannot be excluded, though no mention is made of such a feature.

Προσῳδία also covered the distinction between aspirated and unaspirated vocalic onset in word-initial position («rough» and «smooth breathings»); aspiration, /h/, as a single element was confined to word-initial position in Greek, except for the phonaestetic exclamatory εἶἑν («well») and some pronunciations of the foreign word ταώς «peacock».

One must beware of seeking anticipations of modern concepts in the use of terminological similarities by people working under very different circumstances, but we may observe that, despite some differences of opinion, the scholiasts grouped together under the heading προσῳδία a set of very different phonetic features all associated in one way or another with the syntagmatic dimension in phonology, Sweet's «synthesis» (1877: 56), that dimension with which prosodic phonology is primarily concerned (Bekker 1816: 674-675, 683-684, 702, 705, 709; Palmer 1957; Allen 1973: 3-12).

The main body of the *Technē* is taken up with what one would call today the phonetics and the morphology of classical Greek. The phonetics of Greek was expounded in terms of the pronunciation values of the letters of the alphabet. This was followed by a short passage on syllable structure. The letters, γράμματα, were divided into two major classes, the consonants, σύμφωνα, and the vowels, φωνήεντα; they were simultaneously orthographic and phonological elements, the minimal units of linguistic structure. It is somewhat anachronistic to reproach the Greek linguists for «confusing» the orthographic and phonological levels of analysis; such a separation of levels had not yet been made definitively, and γράμματα were simply the units of articulate speech (ἐγγράμματος φωνή, vocal utterance that could be written down; cp. Abercrombie 1949).

The γράμματα were referred to as στοιχεῖα, elements, and a scholiast reminds us of the threefold character of the linguistic στοιχεῖον that the Stoics had already made explicit, as a written shape, as a named entity (e.g. *alpha*), and as a phonetic value, the *figura, nomen*, and *potestas* of the Latin grammarians (Bekker 1816: 733; Diogenes Laertius VII. 56). This use of στοιχεῖον as the minimal and irreducible element brings Greek linguistics into the pattern of Greek scientific discourse in general, in which the word στοιχεῖον was currently used to refer to the basic constituents of the physical world (cp. Plato, *Theaetētus* 201e, *Politicus* 278d; Aristotle, *Metaphysics* 983b 10, 1014a 26-29). The interpretation of the word made in linguistics by Dionysius may be appropriately compared with Trubetzkoy's definition of the phoneme (1969: 35): «The smallest distinctive unit of a given language».

The *Technē* gives us what was to become the standard inventory of the Greek alphabet as a set of letters with phonetic values, in terms more or less closely reproduced by later Latin accounts of the pronunciation of their language. In general, western antiquity has not been credited with much insight in phonetics (Allen 1981), and reconstructions of the pronunciation of Greek and Latin do not rely on what the ancient authorities wrote to anything like the extent that this can be done with the treatises on the phonetics of Sanskrit (Allen 1953). Perhaps the main reason was that the Greeks adopted an acoustic terminology (from which some traditional terms are derived: *liquid, rough, smooth*, etc.) without the technology to sustain and develop it, such as we have today. The Arabs and the Indians set out articulatory accounts of the sounds of their languages, and in particular it was the Indian phonetic work that provided the real stimulus to European phonetics at the beginning of the nineteenth century when it had become available to Europeans.

The *Technē* deals systematically with the consonants and the vowels, with vowel length, and with syllabic quantity, and notices the three triadic systems, /p/, /p^h/, /b/; /t/, /t^h/, /d/; and /k/, /k^h/, /g/, that made up the classical Greek plosive consonants. The unaspirated and aspirated plosives (as they were, of course, in classical times) were reasonably aligned with the unaspirated and aspirated vocalic onsets as smooth (ψιλά) and rough (δασέα), the latter being specified as having the addition of breath (Bekker 1816: 809). The voiced plosives were called «middle» consonants (μέσα), whence the Latin *mediae* (*litterae*), a term still found in some fairly recent English writers such as Joseph Wright. A great deal of discussion has been devoted to the question of what exactly Dionysius and other Greek writers meant by this term. He glossed it as «rougher than the smooth and smoother than the rough» (Bekker 1816: 631), in some way ranging each set of three consonants along one dimension, whereas we now see that two different contrasts are involved, voice and voicelessness, and aspiration and lack of aspiration (Sanskrit, of course, built a tetradic system from these same contrasts, distinguishing voiced aspirated consonants from voiced unaspirated consonants). It is notorious that Europe as a whole misdiagnosed the feature of voicing until its full explanation, achieved by the ancient Indian phoneticians became known to Europeans (cp. Allen 1974: 28).

Two short sections (§ 12 and § 13) introduce the morphological part of the *Technē*. These take the form of definitions of the two basic units in Greek grammatical description, the word (λέξις) at the lower limit and the sentence (λόγος) at the upper limit. This is followed by a list of the eight word classes, or parts of speech (λόγου μέρη), which are set out in full, with their subclassifications and relevant grammatical categories in the sections that follow.

The word is defined as the smallest unit of syntactic structure (μέρος τοῦ κατὰ σύνταξιν λόγου ἐλάχιστον) and the sentence as a construction expressing a complete thought (λέξεως σύνθεσις διάνοιαν αὐτοτελῆ δηλοῦσα)[10]. This set the pattern for definitions of the sentence that persisted until the time of the Bloomfieldian structuralists with their rigorous exclusion of any such «mentalist» terminology in the establishment of linguistic categories (cp. Fries 1952: 9-16).

[10] In Bekker's text (1816: 634 § 13): «Λόγος δέ ἐστι πεζῆς τε καὶ ἐμμέτρου λέξεως σύνθεσις διάνοιαν αὐτοτελῆ δηλοῦσα». The words καὶ ἐμμέτρου do not appear in the text used by Uhlig, and it has been argued that they were a later addition made in order to include poetry as well as prose within the scope of the definition; but it has been pointed out that πεζός can be used with reference to language to mean «normal», whether of prose or verse. The text of this section has been reexamined recently partly in the light of papyrological evidence by Wouters (1975, 1976; cp. also Pecorella 1962: 103-105), and in the first century papyrus mentioned above the two words in question are not found in the definition of λόγος.

Just as in his phonology Dionysius begins with the minimal units, the γράμματα, and works up to syllables, and, by implication, to syllable groups, so in his grammatical sections he begins with what are for him and for all western antiquity the minimal units of grammar and refers to some of their relations and functions within sentences as logically posterior. In this respect the tradition he followed stands in contrast to the theories of the word and sentence put forward by some of the early Indian grammarians, who insisted on the primacy of the sentence in the analysis of language (Brough 1951: 45-46; 1953).

One notes at once the absence of any mention of a grammatical element corresponding to the modern term *morpheme*; the nearest approach to the concept of a bound morpheme seems to lie in the distinction drawn within compound words between those whose parts are the same in shape as separate words and those whose parts are not but can nevertheless be recognized as recurrent elements of word formation (Bekker 1816: 635). Morphology was handled in antiquity on «word and paradigm» lines, in Hockett's terminology (1954: 210), whereby one form was selected as basic and the forms associated with it were listed in paradigms as the results of κλισις (bending, alteration).

The *Technē* sets out its summary of Greek morphology in twelve sections (§ 14-25) dealing in turn with the eight word classes that were to become the standard set in subsequent grammars of the language. Each class was defined, the categories relevant to its members were then listed, and the various subclasses under each class were then also set out, with examples of each. The brevity and conciseness of the definitions, itself a sign of scientific maturity, may be seen in the eight examples following:

ὄνομα, noun, a class of words inflected for case and signifying a concrete or abstract entity (e.g. stone, education);

ῥῆμα, verb, a class of words not inflected for case, but inflected for tense, person, and number, signifying an action or a being acted on;

μετοχή, participle, sharing the properties of verbs and nouns;

ἄρθρον, article, a class of words inflected for case and preposed or postposed to nouns[11];

ἀντωνυμία, pronoun, a word that serves as a substitute for a noun and is marked for the category of person;

πρόθεσις, preposition, a word that is placed before members of the other word classes both in word formation and in syntax[12];

ἐπίρρημα, adverb, a class of words without inflection modifying or added to a verb;

[11] For this problem, see below, p. 30.

[12] For this problem, see below, p. 28-29.

σύνδεσμος, conjunction, a word binding together and ordering the sentence meaning and filling any gap in its interpretation (this last class included most of the words now called particles in Greek).

This list of eight word classes was the product of the Alexandrian school and it may have been the work of Dionysius's teacher Aristarchus (Lersch 1840: 59-64). But it was Dionysius who formally set it out, and it was on this that his reputation rested (Bekker 1816: 676: «Dionysius Thrax, who taught us about the eight word classes»), and this set the seal on the didactic presentation of grammar in antiquity; Donatus's *Ars minor* (fourth century A.D.) dealt simply with the eight word classes of Latin, and Pompeius, a fifth century Latin grammarian, wrote (Keil ed. 1857-1880: vol. 5, 96): «Qui inchoat artem [sc. grammaticam] debet inchoare ab octo partibus orationis».

We are given a framework of classification in which every item in the lexicon can be assigned a place without ambiguity or overlapping; with a few changes and modifications this framework survives today in the presentation of Greek grammar; it served as the basis for Apollonius's syntactic studies and for the grammars of the later Latin grammarians, and via these for the grammars of the Middle Ages, and for much of the theoretical and practical writing on grammar in the modern world.

Dionysius's set of eight word classes had a long history, which we are able for the most part to retrace through the stages by which it evolved. Plato made a binary division of the sentence (λόγος) into two components, ὄνομα and ῥῆμα, Subject and Predicate or NP and VP (*Cratylus* 425a, 431b; *Sophistēs* 263d). At this early stage these two components were not so much classes of words as sentence constituents. This is the source of the expression μέρος λόγου, part of the sentence; only as the analysis of the sentence and the classification of its words became more detailed and exact did the concept of sentence component develop into that of class of word. But the term remained as part of Greek metalinguistic terminology and was translated into Latin as *pars orationis*; *oratio* also translates as «speech», and traditional grammar has ever since been endowed with this somewhat inappropriate title for word class («part of speech»).

Semantically Plato observed the broad correlation of ὄνομα with the agent and ῥῆμα with the action in many sentences (e.g. *Sophistēs* 262a). But there has been considerable discussion on the inclusion by Plato and later by Aristotle of adjectives and adjectival phrases, such as λευκός «white», Διὶ φίλος «beloved of Zeus», among the ῥήματα, as they share the morphological inflections of nouns, not of verbs (*Cratylus* 399b; *On*

Interpretation 1). It was, however, on syntactic grounds, not by morphological categories, that the first division of the Greek sentence had been made, and in Greek sentences adjectives often served as predicates without a copula necessarily present, as in λευκός ὁ ἵππος «the horse (is) white»; that is, they could stand alone in the ῥῆμα place. It is to be remembered that one is dealing here not with questions of the use or the misuse of an existing technical metalanguage, but with the very early stages in the working out of such a metalanguage from the material available in a language not hitherto put to such a purpose.

In Aristotle's writings on language we find the first explicit treatment of grammatically relevant word form variations that were later to be collected and ordered in the familiar paradigms. He used the word πτῶσις, literally meaning «fall», and later to be translated into the Latin *casus*, to refer to such variations. At this stage πτῶσις was used indifferently for any variations of word forms, which were regarded as deviations from a descriptively basic form. Aristotle thus distinguished the oblique cases of nouns and the non-present tense forms of verbs as πτώσεις ὀνόματος and πτώσεις ῥήματος respectively; and comparative and superlative forms of adjectives, and deadjectival adverbs like δίκαιως «justly», were also referred to as πτώσεις (*On Interpretation* 2, 3; *Topics* 5.7, 2.9, 1.15)[13].

Several writers attribute to Aristotle the recognition of a third set of sentence components, the σύνδεσμοι «binders», to which he assigned what were later distinguished as conjunctions, articles, and pronouns, their function being to ensure the unity of the sentence as a single whole (Aristotle, *Rhetoric* 3.5, 3.12; Dionysius of Halicarnassus, *de compositione verborum* 2, *de vi Demosthenis*, 48). At this stage in the evolution of grammatical analysis one need not wonder at Aristotle's alleged «failure» to make further distinctions within the σύνδεσμοι. Certainly the personal pronouns serve very different purposes from those served by the rest of Aristotle's σύνδεσμοι; but in Greek, as there was no grammatical requirement for an overt subject, their occurrence was stylistic or emphatic, not essential, and they did not, therefore, constitute a necessary component of a complete sentence[14].

[13] There has been considerable discussion of the genesis of the word πτῶσις as a technical term in Greek grammatical metalanguage; see Hiersche et al. (1955) and Murru (1980). The word, which in non-technical usage meant «fall», was also used by Aristotle as a technical term in logic (*Prior analytics* 1. 26, 42b 30; *Posterior analytics* 2. 10, 94a 12).

[14] This removes the force of Lersch's argument (1840: 16-17) that a thinker of the status of Aristotle must have recognized the article as a separate class in its own right. The alleged

The separate recognition of the ἄρθρον, to include all the inflected members of Aristotle's class of σύνδεσμοι, i.e. the later definite article, relative pronoun, and personal pronouns, was the work of the Stoics. They used the term στοιχεῖον «element», to refer to words as components of sentences, and it is from the time of the Stoics that the grammarians can be seen to be dealing explicitly with word classes, defined and distinguished by their specific morphological categories and syntactic functions, rather than with more indeterminately sized sentence components, though the expression μέρος λόγου continued in use, as does its English successor, *part of speech*.

The Stoics whose philosophical attitude led them to give linguistics, and specifically grammar, a place of its own in their system, made a major advance in the articulation of grammatical description by restricting πτῶσις to the inflections of nouns and other words inflected like nouns; from now on it is legitimate to translate πτῶσις by «case» in its traditional usage. The Stoic ἄρθρον class was case-inflected; the σύνδεσμοι that were left were all uninflected. Now, too, there was a clear categorial distinction between noun and verb, with the adjective firmly within the noun (ὄνομα) class. Stoic grammarians made a particular study of the case system; nominatives were now counted along with the oblique forms as cases, and, indeed, it was they who made the syntactic distinction between the «upright» case (πτῶσις ὀρθή or εὐθεῖα) constructed with active verb forms (Σωκράτης περιπάτει «Socrates walks») and the «sideways» or oblique cases (πτώσεις πλάγιαι) constructed mainly as the extension of transitive verbs (Πλάτων Διώνα φίλει «Plato loves Dion»; Πλάτων ἀκούει Σωκράτους «Plato listens to Socrates»); and construction with an oblique case was the criterion applied by the Stoics for identifying transitive verbs (Diogenes Laertius VII. 64; cp. Apollonius, *de constructione* III. 32 (295), in Householder's translation pp. 222-223).

The first Stoic system was thus fourfold. At a later stage Diogenes and

Aristotelian passages which seem to refer to ἄρθρον in its later meaning of «article» are highly suspect (Steinthal's treatment of this question [1890-1891²: vol. I, 263-266] is conclusive). Koller's proposal (1958: 28-29) that Aristotle's σύνδεσμος simply meant the copula, uniting ὄνομα and ῥῆμα in a proposition, cannot be reconciled with the majority of passages where the word appears and flies in the face of Dionysius of Halicarnassus's statement that the Stoics separated their ἄρθρα from the σύνδεσμοι of Aristotle (*de compositione verborum* 2). It must be recalled that at this time in the development of linguistic analysis it would be anachronistic to look for the sort of precision in grammatical terms that is to be found in later systems, in which the recognition of more technical terms has made such precision possible.

Chrysippus divided the ὄνομα class into two, ὄνομα «proper noun», and προσηγορία «common noun». The distinction was based on the semantic contrast between individual quality (ἴδια ποιότης) and shared quality (κοινὴ ποιότης), though this was implausibly linked with a difference of inflection, Πάρις, Πάριδος, as against μάντις, μάντεως («prophet»); this formal criterion obviously will not work, in view of many common nouns like φροντίς, φροντίδος («thought»), but once more we are seeing here the process of trying out different possibilities that might suggest themselves (Diogenes Laertius VII. 57-58; Bekker 1816: 842; Priscian, *Institutiones* II. 16).

In a further modification of the Stoic system, Antipater is said to have introduced a sixth word class, the μεσότης, probably comprising the adverbs in -ως; this was the term for this group as a later subclass within the ἐπίρρημα (adverb) class (Diogenes Laertius VII. 57; Bekker 1816: 641 § 24). Other Stoics referred to adverbs by the term πανδέκτης; the technical etymology of this word is obscure, but conceivably it might be the result of widening the class to include all words syntactically equivalent to the adverbs in -ως (πανδέκτης «the all-receiver»), the membership of the subsequent ἐπίρρημα class.

The final system, set out in the *Technē*, involved the recognition of three further classes, the pronoun, the participle, and the preposition, and the reinclusion of the proper and common nouns as subclasses of the single ὄνομα class, a change explicitly noticed by Dionysius (Bekker 1816: 634). This last change became part of the standard presentation of the word classes in the Graeco-Roman tradition. But its specific mention here may be due to still current divergences of treatment even outside the Stoic schools, as an Egyptian papyrus from the first century A.D. (Wouters 1979: 49) maintains the ὄνομα and the προσηγορία in separate classes.

The evolution of the Dionysian system may be tabulated diagrammatically as in the scheme on p. 26.

Under several of the word classes very comprehensive lists of subclasses are given, in both formal and semantic terms (e.g. compound nouns and verbs; local and interrogative adverbs); but no mention is made of irregular forms and suppletive paradigms, which are very numerous in ancient Greek. Such irregularities would not invalidate the classifications and subclassifications; they would constitute «anomalies», and consequently the statement of such forms would not be part of the «working out of regularities» (ἀναλογίας ἐκλογισμός). The word

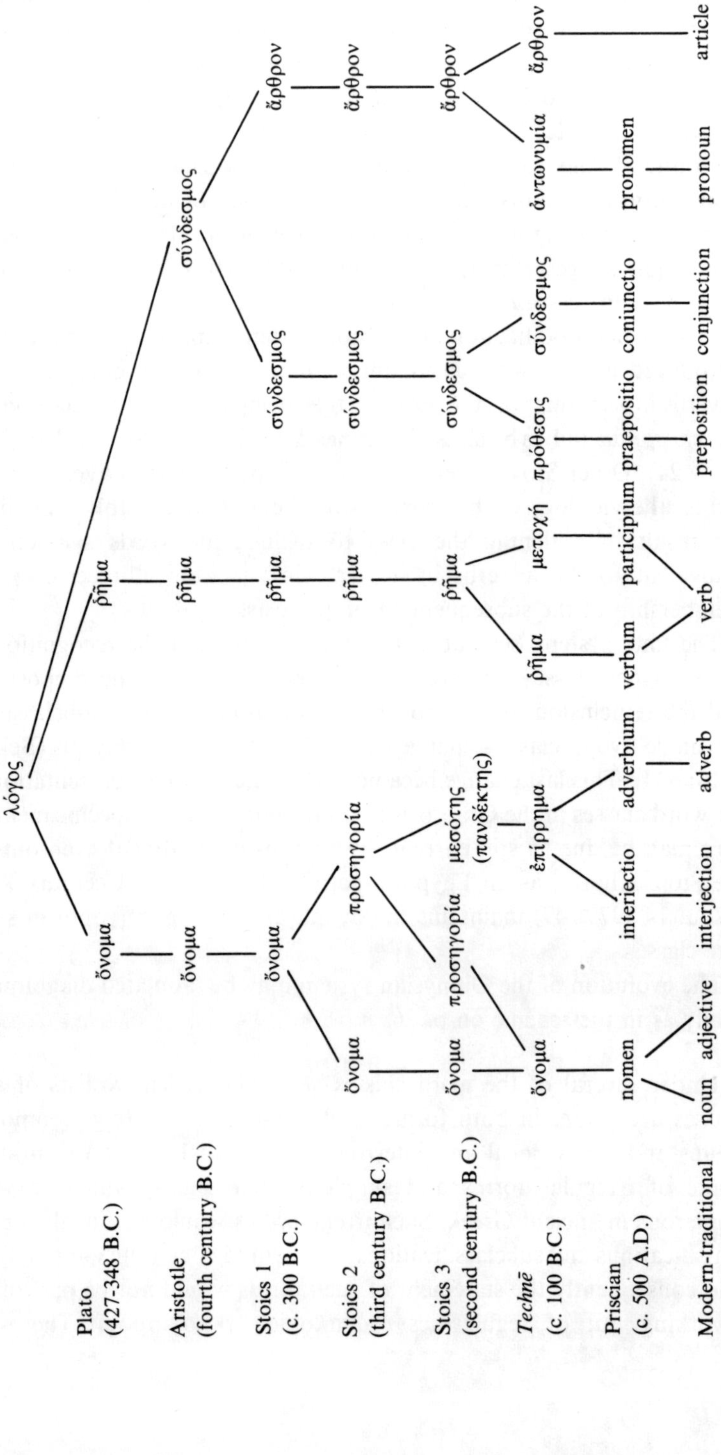
Plato (427-348 B.C.)
λόγος
ὄνομα
ῥῆμα
Aristotle (fourth century B.C.)
ὄνομα
ῥῆμα
σύνδεσμος
Stoics 1 (c. 300 B.C.)
ὄνομα
ῥῆμα
σύνδεσμος
ἄρθρον
Stoics 2 (third century B.C.)
ὄνομα
προσηγορία
ῥῆμα
σύνδεσμος
ἄρθρον
Stoics 3 (second century B.C.)
ὄνομα
προσηγορία
μεσότης (πανδέκτης)
ῥῆμα
σύνδεσμος
ἄρθρον
Technē (c. 100 B.C.)
ὄνομα
ἐπίρρημα
ῥῆμα
μετοχή
πρόθεσις
σύνδεσμος
ἀντωνυμία
ἄρθρον
Priscian (c. 500 A.D.)
nomen
interiectio
adverbium
verbum
participium
praepositio
coniunctio
pronomen
Modern-traditional
noun
adjective
interjection
adverb
verb
preposition
conjunction
pronoun
article

classes and their grammatical categories as set out in the *Technē* differ so little from those used today in the teaching of classical Greek and, indeed, in most traditional teaching of modern languages, that comment can be reserved for those points at which there is divergence between the *Technē* and modern usage.

The most prominent differences are the status accorded to the participle as a separate word class and the place of the adjective as a subclass of nouns instead of in a class of its own.

The participle was the subject of considerable attention in antiquity, but it preserved its separate status in both Greek and Latin grammars up to the end of the Middle Ages (Lersch 1840: 130-131; Steinthal 1890-1891^{2}: vol. II, 216-218; Kukenheim 1951: 20-21, 61). Such a treatment is uneconomical (as was noted by a scholiast, Bekker 1816: 896), since the membership of the two classes of verb and participle stand in a fixed numerical relation to each other, but the position accorded to the participle is understandable and defensible. The noun and the verb had been defined as case-inflected and non-case-inflected, respectively, but the participle inflected for both categories; and the participle contracts the nominal concords of gender, number and case within nominal endocentric groups, and verbal government (rection) of oblique cases within what would today be called an embedded VP construction, as well as exhibiting in Greek (unlike its Latin counterpart) a full range of tense distinctions in the active, middle, and passive voices. This synthesis or «sharing» of the morphological and syntactic features of nouns and verbs was expressed in the Greek word μετοχή, directly translated into the Latin *participium*.

The status of the adjective as a subclass of the noun (which is echoed today by those who still speak of *noun substantive* and *noun adjective*) was more in agreement with the morphology of Greek, in which adjectives shared all the inflectional categories of nouns, than in a language like modern English. The principal formal differentia of adjectives, the paradigm of comparative and superlative forms, was in effect made unavailable to Dionysius as a criterion, by the fact that these forms were themselves treated as subclasses of the noun class (ὀνόματα συγκριτικά and ὀνόματα ὑπερθετικά).

The categories applicable to the various word classes, and on which were based any morphological subclassifications, were referred to as παρεπόμενα, «accompanying features», and in listing and defining them no distinction was drawn between derivational and inflectional formations, a rather general tendency in antiquity. Dionysius's treatment of these categories can be illustrated from those ascribed to the noun and verb classes: gender, type, form, number, and case in nouns, and mood, voice, type, form, number, tense, person, and conjugation in verbs. Two of the categories shared by nouns and verbs, type (εἶδος) and form (σχῆμα), relate to the morphemic structure of the words concerned; there were two types, primary and derived, γῆ «earth», and γαιήιος «of the earth», and ἄρδω and ἀρδεύω, both meaning «to water», being given as examples; three forms were distinguished: simple, compound, and derived from a compound: in nouns, Μέμνων, Φιλόδημος, and Φιλιππίδης («descendant of Philip»), and in verbs, φρονῶ «to think», καταφρονῶ «to despise», and φιλιππίζω «to take the side of Philip».

The other categories very largely corresponded with their present-day counterparts, though there are some differences in the way that one or two were applied. In the category of case Dionysius lists the five cases with their Greek names, which have become part of traditional grammatical terminology *via* Latin. Probably the Stoics had excluded the vocative from their case system as being syntactically unlike the other four; if so, Chrysippus, who wrote «On the five cases» (Diogenes Laertius VII. 192) must have treated deadjectival adverbs in -ως as a πτῶσις (as had Aristotle in his much wider use of the word), to be accorded separate class status as μεσότης by Antipater and the later Stoics (Steinthal 1890-1891^{2}: vol. I, 302). Dionysius's inclusion of the vocative among the cases rests primarily on giving preference to morphological criteria in grammatical analysis and description. Vocative forms of case-inflected words, where they differ from nominatives, are conveniently treated as part of the inflectional case paradigms. Their exclusion from case systems must be justified either on semantic grounds, that case is primarily the grammatical expression of a relationship between the case-marked word and some other constituent of the sentence and that the vocative expresses no such relationship (cp. Hjelmslev 1935: 4, 96), or on syntactic grounds that all other case forms contract specific syntactic relations with other words, whereas vocatives generally stand out as semi-independent interjection-like elements (προσαγορευτικὰ πράγματα, as the Stoics called them; Diogenes Laertius VII. 67).

One would not dispute Dionysius's establishment of the separate classes of preposition and adverb, though his definitions of these are somewhat discrepant from their actual functions in Greek sentences. He says that the preposition (Bekker 1816: 641 § 23) is preposed to members of other word classes in word formation and in syntax, thus identifying prepositions as words with the etymologically related morphemes within some complex words (μετατίθημι «to change», σύμπας «all, together», and ἀνάπαυλα «repose», could be given as examples). But we must bear in mind the rather looser connection between such morphemes and the verb stems in compound verbs, where, as a scholiast observes (Bekker 1816: 927), the past tense augment normally comes between the prepositional morpheme and the verb stem (as in προσέβαινον «they were approaching»). This misleading and inadequate definition of the preposition was repeated almost word for word by Priscian in his Latin definition. The central function of this class of words in Latin and in Greek of linking nouns and noun phrases to verbs was identified by the mediaeval grammarians and this was an important achievement (cp. Bursill-Hall 1972: 264).

It seems hard to account for the statement implicit in Dionysius's definition and repeated throughout antiquity that the adverb is always directly associated syntactically with a verb. No notice appears to have been taken of constructions in which such adverbs as μᾶλλον «more», πάνυ «wholly», and λίαν «too much» (all listed by Dionysius) are generally linked with an adjective or another adverb. In this respect the analogy drawn by a scholiast (Bekker 1816: 932) between adjective and substantive (ἐπίθετον ὄνομα and other subclasses of ὄνομα) and adverb and verb (ἐπίρρημα and ῥῆμα) breaks down.

The designation of one of the subclasses of adverb requires notice. Those formed from adjectival stems and ending in -ως are referred to as μεσότητος παραστατικά, exponents of what lies in the middle. This name for the most productive class of adverbs goes back to the Stoics. Its origin is hard to trace; Lersch (1840: 44-46) suggests that these words, morphologically associated with nouns (of which adjectives were a subclass) but syntactically linked to verbs, were regarded as lying «midway» between these two major classes.

Adverbs, prepositions, and conjunctions were distinguished from the other five word classes by their lack of inflection (comparative and superlative adverbs were simply adverbs in their own right). Dionysius includes the term ἄκλιτον, uninflected, in his definition of the adverb; the scholiasts add it to their definitions of the other two (Bekker 1816: 641, 924, 952).

Dionysius distinguished three of his classes as closed, that is, classes whose membership could be listed and did not readily admit of new members. The three classes were prepositions, conjunctions, and the article. In the *Technē* the members of each class are given in lists. The article class, ἄρθρον, comprised two members, the definite article, and what we know today as the relative pronoun, distinguished as preposed (προτασσόμενον) and postposed (ὑποτασσόμενον); the two sets of word forms were morphologically associated in Greek (ὁ, ἡ, τό; ὅς, ἥ, ὅ, etc.). Latin had no equivalent to the article, and Latin grammarians classed their relative pronouns (*qui, quae, quod*, etc.) with nouns (or in the case of a few writers, with pronouns). Latin morphology associates relative and interrogative words, and Dionysius treated Greek interrogatives (τίς «who?», ποῖος «of what sort?», etc.) as a subclass of nouns (ὀνόματα ἐρωτηματικά). Dionysius separated the pronouns from within the ἄρθρον class of the Stoics by their specification of person, and in general the Greek and the Latin grammarians confined membership of the pronoun class to the personal and the possessive pronouns (ἐγώ, σύ, ἐμός, σός, etc.).

The only Latin innovation among the word classes was the interjection, a class of words which had been included among the adverbs by the Greek grammarians, except for ὦ, which was ingeniously identified as the vocative of the definite article by Dionysius (ὦ Ζεῦ «oh Zeus!», etc.).

The most conspicuous gap in the *Technē* is the absence of any treatment of the syntax of Greek, and modern scholars have not failed to point this out. The systematic presentation of the syntactic structures of Greek sentences was effected some two and a half centuries later by Apollonius Dyscolus, and his work provided the model, explicitly acknowledged, for Priscian's comprehensive grammar of Latin (Priscian, *Institutiones* XII. 13, XIV. 1, XVI. 1), which in turn formed the basis for the grammatical tradition of western Europe. It may be noted that the morphological descriptions and classifications made in the *Technē* were taken over by Apollonius, who must be regarded as having built on this prior work rather than as having corrected or superseded it. The morphology and the grammatical categories set out in the *Technē* were a suitable basis for the analysis of sentence structure, and it is clear that the investigation of syntactic questions was part of the context in which the Alexandrian grammarians worked; the basic unit of grammar, λέξις, the word, was defined syntactically, and some of the word classes and their subclasses were wholly or partly defined in syntactic terms.

The scholiasts in their comments on the *Technē* naturally concentrate their attention on morphological questions, but they also add to Dionysius's statements with syntactic observations. They draw attention, for example, to the following points: the different case concord of the ἄρθρον προτασσόμενον, the modern definite article, and the ἄρθρον ὑποτασσόμενον, the modern relative pronoun, the former always agreeing with the case of its following noun, the latter taking its case from the syntax of its own clause; the possibility of a formal definition of person in the personal pronouns by reference to the verb inflections used with their nominative forms; the double concord of the possessive pronouns, of the stem with the possessor and of the inflection with the possessed; the positional restrictions on certain of the σύνδεσμος class, mostly falling in the modern set of particles, to non-initial place in the sentence or clause; and the important difference between the positional relations of individual words in a sentence and the syntactic relations between them as members of word classes exhibiting specific grammatical categories (Bekker 1816: 900, 909, 913-914, 935, 958-960).

The Stoics are known to have written specifically on syntax and to have worked out a form of syntactic theory in fairly abstract terms (cp. Long ed. 1971; Mates 1953). Unfortunately, none of the primary sources survive and it is now difficult to reconstruct their syntactic theory in any detail. In any case it appears that it was not taken up widely outside Stoic schools and it does not form part of the main stream of grammatical teaching; Priscian is aware of Stoic work and he refers to it in places, but briefly and sporadically without in any way integrating it into his own exposition.

It is possible to suggest a reason for the priority given to inventories of word classes and subclasses, separate paradigms, sets of categories, and class meanings. Almost all branches of knowledge in later antiquity lay under the influence of Aristotle's massive and comprehensive codification of Greek logic and Greek scientific method. Aristotle's actual grammatical work was incidental and relatively rudimentary but the analogist theory of language, to which the Alexandrians, but not the Stoics, subscribed, was directly grounded in Aristotelian doctrine, and one will better understand the method and the outlook of Dionysius and his commentators within the context of Aristotelian scientific method, dominated as it was by the primary aim of achieving adequate and accurate definitions. At the outset of the *Technē* Dionysius lays down the definition of his subject, as a commentator points out, in thoroughly Aristotelian terms. One may compare his definition of grammar with Aristotle's statement that «Definition is of the distinctive nature and essence of something»[15]. Dionysius's grammatical procedure is clearly

[15] Aristotle, *Posterior analytics* 2. 3, 90b 30-31: «ὁρισμὸς μὲν γὰρ τοῦ τί ἐστι καὶ

modelled on the scientific procedure set out by Aristotle with statements by reference to genus, differentia, property, and accident (cp. *Topics* 1. 4, 101b, 17-25). We may compare Dionysius's treatment of the word classes (λόγου μέρη) with the principles of Aristotle's analytic method:

«When one is dealing with a subject in its entirety one must divide the species into its minimal constituents and then in this way try to grasp their definitions»[16].

Each word class is defined by one or more qualitative or relational features predicable of it entirely and exclusively; the class is then subdivided on similar lines into various subclasses, wherever this is possible. With this one may compare Aristotle's statement (*Topics* 1. 5: 102a, 31):

«Genus is that which is predicable of the essential nature of several things which differ in kind (εἶδος)».

In the *Technē* εἶδος is generally used to designate a specific formal subclassification, that of primary *versus* derived word form, but it is also used in the Aristotelian sense for subclass in general in the section on adverbs (§ 24), in the statement that common nouns (προσηγορίαι) are a subclass of nouns (ὀνόματα, § 13), and in a further list of subclasses (εἴδη, Bekker 1816: 636-637)[17].

The various grammatical categories applicable to members of the word classes are given as the παρεπόμενα «consequential attributes», of each; and a commentator, seeing the Aristotelian form of the analysis, interpreted παρεπόμενον as συμβεβηκός «accidents», to be contrasted with the properties, ἴδια, of each, peculiar to each class and so forming part of its definition[18].

οὐσίας»; cp. 2. 9, 93b 29. Scholiast in Bekker (1816: 647): «Ἀριστοτέλης οὖν οὕτως ὁρίζεται τὸν ὅρον· ὅρος ἐστὶν ὁ τὸ τί εἶναι δηλῶν».

[16] *Posterior analytics* 2. 13, 96b 15-18: «χρὴ δέ, ὅταν ὅλον τι πραγματεύηταί τις, διελεῖν τὸ γένος εἰς τὰ ἄτομα ... εἶθ' οὕτως ἐκείνων ὁρισμοὺς πειρᾶσθαι λαμβάνειν».

[17] This latter passage, suspected by Steinthal (1890-1891²: vol. II, 250-251), is accepted by Uhlig, and is, in any case, consistent with the grammatical method of the *Technē*. Each word class, of course, while itself constituting a γένος, is a subaltern γένος in relation to the larger γένος of the set of word classes of the language, the form in which the grammar of the language is envisaged for analysis.

[18] Bekker (1816: 843, 845-846); cp. Aristotle, *Topics* 1. 5, 102b 4-6. For the use of the term παρεπόμενον by Aristotle in a similar sense, cp. *Sophistical refutations* 168b 28-31, *Topics* 4. 6, 128a 38; 5. 3, 131a 27.
As has been seen, the feature of case inflection itself is an ἴδιον, a particular property and part of the definition of the noun and of some other classes, but it is an «accident» (παρεπόμενον, συμβεβηκός) for the word to be in any specific case form. This distinction applies equally to the other terms appearing both as grammatical categories, παρεπόμενα,

The application of these Aristotelian principles to linguistic analysis was bound to lead to the breakdown of the material of discourse into classes of minimal elements that can be separately defined and distinguished, words in grammar and letters or phonemes (γράμματα) in phonetics. We are, in fact, given an inventory of the Greek language, lists of its constituent parts at two levels. This is not the whole story that we need to know; we want to see how the parts fit together in the structures of sentences. But what is set down and established in the *Technē* represented a very long step in the right direction, and its phonological and morphological descriptive inventories became the accepted basis for the later syntactic analyses.

To speak of the system of Dionysius as established is not to imply that in the ensuing tradition no changes were made. Some minor amendments were put into the scholiasts' comments, and we have already noticed the reallocation of his ἄρθρον ὑποτασσόμενον to the noun class in Latin grammarians, and the Latin innovation of a separate interjection class. But the descriptive framework of eight classes remained, and the grammatical categories taken as criterial were not altered, though they were differently applied in some details. Indeed, so much was Priscian's treatment of the word classes of Latin, which was itself taken from Apollonius and Dionysius, left unchallenged, that when in the later Middle Ages the speculative grammarians placed quite a different interpretation on Latin grammar it was never thought necessary to call in question the classes and categories themselves. Any such challenge had to await Renaissance grammatical work, but even after this the modern treatments of Greek and Latin grammar, and of the grammar of several other languages, though differing in certain respects for example in treating participles as part of the inflections of the verb and allotting adjectives to a class of their own, do not depart radically from the classificatory and categorial system set out in the *Technē* more than two thousand years ago.

The importance of the Dionysian tradition was recognized early in the non-Greek Middle East. The *Technē* was translated into Syriac and into Armenian, and the grammatical work following from it was itself influential in the shaping of the linguistic scholarship of the Arabic grammarians. Arabic linguistics began independently, in response to the

and as part of the definition of a word class. Priscian and the other Latin grammarians translated παρεπόμενα by *accidentia*, and this is the source of the English *accidence* to designate the inflectional aspect of grammar.

secular and religious needs that arose with the Islamic conquests from the seventh century onward; and Arabic scholars maintained their own independent development, but there are clear traces of conceptual and terminological borrowing, that must have arisen from a familiarity with Greek linguistic teaching and a recognition of its scientific value (Versteegh 1977, 1980).

Modern logic is now far removed from the logic of Aristotle, though that remained master of its field almost until modern times; and modern science is still further away from the science of the Ionian and other Greek scientific pioneers. But in these spheres our predecessors are not thought the less of for that, and an account and evaluation of their work finds a proper place in a general survey of the history of logic and of scientific procedure. Dionysius Thrax's *Technē* and the whole tradition of Greek and Latin grammatical scholarship that it made possible stand at least as good a comparison with present-day linguistics as do the works of Greek writers in other intellectual fields in relation to their successors today. It is reasonable to claim for the *Technē* the attention both of classical scholars and of linguists, as being not the least of the intellectual achievements of the ancient world and a notable stage in the history of linguistics. In that history we have no cause to dissent from the judgment of the scholiast that Dionysius's establishment of the eight word classes was his most important single contribution.

References

Abercrombie, D. 1949. «What is a letter?». *Lingua* 2. 54-63.

Allen, W.S. 1948. «Ancient ideas on the origin and development of language». *Transactions of the Philological Society* 1948. 35-60.

Allen, W.S. 1953. *Phonetics in Ancient India.* London: Oxford University Press.

Allen, W.S. 1973. *Accent and rhythm: prosodic features of Latin and Greek. A study in theory and reconstruction.* Cambridge: University Press.

Allen, W.S. 1974. *Vox graeca.* Cambridge: University Press.

Allen, W.S. 1981. «The Greek contribution to the history of phonetics». R.E. Asher - E. Henderson eds., *Towards a history of phonetics: Papers contributed in honour of David Abercrombie*, 115-122. Edinburgh: University Press.

Apollonius Dyscolus [second century A.D.]. *Syntax* (transl. F.W. Householder; Amsterdam: J. Benjamins, 1981).

Aristotle [384-322 B.C.]. *Metaphysics; Nicomachean ethics; On interpretation; Physics; Posterior analytics; Prior analytics; Rhetoric; Sophistical refutations; Topics.*

Athenaeus [c. 200 A.D.]. *Deipnosophistae.*

Bekker, I. 1816. *Anecdota graeca*, vol. 2. Berlin: Reimer.
Brough, J. 1951. «Theories of general linguistics in the Sanskrit grammarians». *Transactions of the Philological Society* 1951. 27-46.
Brough, J. 1953. «Some Indian theories of meaning». *Transactions of the Philological Society* 1953. 161-176.
Bursill-Hall, G.L. 1972. *Thomas of Erfurt: Grammatica speculativa. An edition with translation and commentary*. London: Longman.
Bury, J.B. 1923. *The Hellenistic age*. Cambridge: University Press.
Chomsky, N. 1964. *Current issues in linguistic theory*. The Hague: Mouton.
Chomsky, N. 1979. *Language and responsibility*. Hassocks: Harvester Press.
Classen, J. 1829. *De grammaticae graecae primordiis*. Bonn: C.F. Thurmann.
Collart, J. 1954. *Varron, grammairien latin*. Paris: Les Belles Lettres.
Colson, F.H. 1919. «The analogist and anomalist controversy». *Classical Quarterly* 13. 24-36.
Di Benedetto, V. 1958-1959. «Dionisio Trace e la Techne a lui attribuita». *Annali della Scuola Normale Superiore di Pisa*, serie 2, 27. 169-210; 28. 87-118.
Diogenes Laertius [c. 200-250 A.D.]. *Lives and opinions of eminent philosophers*.
Donatus [fourth century A.D.]. *Ars maior; Ars minor*.
Forbes, P.B.R. 1933. «Greek pioneers in philology and grammar». *The Classical Review* 47. 105-112.
Fries, C.C. 1952. *The structure of English*. New York: Harcourt Brace.
Funaioli, H. 1907. *Grammaticorum romanorum fragmenta*. Leipzig: Teubner.
Gellius, Aulus [second century A.D.]. *Noctes atticae*.
Hiersche, R. et al. 1955. *Entstehung und Entwicklung des Terminus πτῶσις*. (Sitzungsberichte der Deutschen Akademie der Wissenschaften, 3). Berlin: Akademie.
Hjelmslev, L. 1935-1937. *La catégorie des cas. Étude de grammaire générale*. (Acta Jutlandica 7:1; 9:2).
Hockett, C.F. 1954. «Two models of grammatical description». *Word* 10. 210-234.
Keil, H. ed. 1857-1880. *Grammatici latini*. Leipzig: Teubner (Repr. Hildesheim: G. Olms, 1961).
Koller, H. 1958. «Die Anfänge der griechischen Grammatik». *Glotta* 37. 5-40.
Kukenheim, L. 1951. *Contributions à l'histoire de la grammaire grecque, latine et hébraïque à l'époque de la Renaissance*. Leiden: Brill.
Lersch, L. 1840. *Die Sprachphilosophie der Alten*, II. Teil. Bonn: H.B. König (Repr. Hildesheim: G. Olms, 1971).
Liddell, H.G. - R. Scott. 1940[9]. *A Greek-English lexicon*. Oxford: Clarendon Press.
Long, A.A. ed. 1971. *Problems in stoicism*. London: Athlone Press.
Mates, B. 1953. *Stoic logic*. Berkeley: University Press.
Murru, F. 1980. «Due note di storia della linguistica antica». *Münchener Studien zur Sprachwissenschaft* 39. 73-84.
Origen [185-254 A.D.]. *Against Celsus*.
Palmer, F.R. ed. 1970. *Prosodic analysis*. London: Oxford University Press.

Palmer, L.R. 1957. «Some observations on the language of linguists». E. Pulgram ed., *Studies presented to Joshua Whatmough*, 187-192. The Hague: Mouton.

Pauly, A.G. - G. Wissowa. 1893-1972. *Paulys Realencyclopädie der classischen Altertumswissenschaft*. Stuttgart: J.B. Metzler.

Pecorella, G.B. 1962. *Dionisio Trace. ΤΕΧΝΗ ΓΡΑΜΜΑΤΙΚΗ. Testo critico e commento*. Bologna: Cappelli.

Pfeiffer, R. 1968. *History of classical scholarship*. Oxford: University Press.

Pinborg, J. 1975. «Classical antiquity: Greece». T.A. Sebeok ed., *Current trends in linguistics*, vol. 13: *Historiography of Linguistics* (ass. eds. H. Aarsleff, R. Austerlitz, D. Hymes, E. Stankiewicz), 69-126. The Hague-Paris: Mouton.

Plato [c. 427-348 B.C.]. *Cratylus; Gorgias; Politicus; Sophistēs; Theaetētus.*

Priscian [c. 500 A.D.]. *Institutiones grammaticae.*

Robins, R.H. 1974. «Theory-orientation versus data-orientation». *Historiographia Linguistica* 1. 11-26.

Robins, R.H. 1976. «Varro and the tactics of analogist grammarians». A. Morpurgo Davies - W. Meid eds., *Studies in Greek, Italic, and Indo-European linguistics offered to Leonard R. Palmer*, 333-336. Innsbruck: Institut für Sprachwissenschaft.

Robins, R.H. 1979[2]. *A short history of linguistics*. London: Longman (1967[1]).

Sandys, Sir John Edwin. 1920[3]. *History of classical scholarship*, vol. I. Cambridge: Cambridge University Press (1903[1]).

Schmidt, M. 1852-1853. «Dionys der Thraker». *Philologus* 7. 360-382; 8. 231-253, 510-520.

Sextus Empiricus [third century A.D.]. *Against the grammarians.*

Steinthal, H. 1890-1891[2]. *Geschichte der Sprachwissenschaft bei den Griechen und Römern, mit besonderer Rücksicht auf die Logik* (1863[1]; repr. Hildesheim: G. Olms, 1971).

Susemihl, F. 1891-1892. *Geschichte der Griechischen Literatur in der Alexandrinerzeit*. Leipzig: Teubner.

Sweet, H. 1877. *A handbook of phonetics*. Oxford: Clarendon Press.

Traglia, A. 1956. «La sistemazione grammaticale di Dionisio Trace». *Studi classici ed orientali* 15. 38-78.

Trubetzkoy, N.S. 1969. *Principles of phonology* (transl. C.A.M. Baltaxe). Berkeley: University of California Press (originally published in German: *Grundzüge der Phonologie*, 1939).

Uhlig, G. 1883. *Dionysii Tracis ars grammatica*. Leipzig: Teubner.

Varro [first century B.C.]. *De lingua latina.*

Versteegh, C.H.M. 1977. *Greek elements in Arabic linguistic thinking*. Leiden: Brill.

Versteegh, C.H.M. 1980. «Hellenistic education and the origin of Arabic grammar». K. Koerner ed., *Progress in linguistic historiography*, 333-344. Amsterdam: J. Benjamins.

Wouters, A. 1975. «Dionysius Thrax' definition of the ΛΟΓΟΣ (sentence) and P. Yale I 25». *Orbis* 24. 217-223.

Wouters, A. 1976. «De papyri en de geschiedenis van de grammaticale wetenschap in de Oudheid». *Handelingen der Koninklijke Zuidnederlandse Maatschappij voor Taal- en Letterkunde en Geschiedenis* 30. 291-307.

Wouters, A. 1979. *The grammatical papyri from Graeco-Roman Egypt. Contributions to the study of the «ars grammatica» in Antiquity*. Brussel: Paleis der Academiën.

Pierre SWIGGERS
(F.N.R.S. belge)

MOT ET PARTIE DU DISCOURS DANS LA GRAMMAIRE FRANÇAISE AUX XVIIe ET XVIIIe SIÈCLES

0. L'âge classique est, à plus d'un égard, une époque intéressante pour l'historien de la grammaire (ou de la linguistique)[1]: c'est l'époque à laquelle la grammaire des langues «vernaculaires» se libère du joug latin, en reconnaissant la variété et la diversité des langues[2]. Cette évolution dans le sens d'une théorisation[3] a eu des effets salubres pour le développement de la syntaxe[4], assurant l'autonomisation de la grammaire française à l'égard du modèle latin. Les efforts conjugués des grammairiens visent à l'organisation de la grammaire comme une discipline basée sur des principes cognitifs. Le modèle latin, s'il est maintenu dans le domaine de la morpho-syntaxe (les parties du discours), est inséré dans un contexte global, celui de l'analyse philosophique des catégories grammaticales (cf. *infra*). On s'attend donc à voir définie la notion de mot en tant qu'unité linguistique. Or, la grammaire française n'offre aucune définition linguistique du mot: le plus souvent, les grammairiens ne se soucient guère de définir le mot, et dans les rares cas où l'on propose une définition, celle-ci est philosophique et/ou sémiotique. Ainsi, de Port-Royal à l'*Encyclopédie* (qui contient un long article «Mot»)[5], le mot est défini comme le signe de notre pensée: «sons distincts & articulez dont les hommes ont fait des signes pour signifier leurs pensées» (*Grammaire* II, 1, p. 27); «totalité de sons devenue par usage, pour ceux qui l'entendent, le signe d'une idée totale» (Mot, *E.M.*, tome II, p. 583). Si l'on peut encore comprendre le manque de précision

[1] Pour le point de vue des historiens de la philosophie, voir Foucault (1966) et Robinet (1978).

[2] Sur l'histoire de la grammaire française, on consultera Loiseau (1875), Harnois (1928), Chevalier (1968: 420 sv.); pour le XVIIe siècle, voir Swiggers (éd. 1984). Sur «l'ouverture» aux langues et dialectes modernes, et à l'histoire des usages linguistiques, voir Droixhe (1978). Pour l'histoire de la grammaire anglaise, voir Michael (1970) et Vorlat (1975). Sur la persistance de la grammaire latine, voir Padley (1976).

[3] Voir, pour la tradition française, Auroux (1979) et Swiggers (1984a).

[4] Cf. Chevalier (1968), Swiggers (1983d; 1984a: 106-140), et Dominicy (1984).

[5] Voir *Encyclopédie méthodique* (abréviation *E.M.*), tome II, p. 570-585.

et de détail chez les auteurs de la *Grammaire* de Port-Royal — les principes explicatifs qu'ils formulent ont avant tout une portée pédagogique[6] —, il n'en va pas de même pour les encyclopédistes: comme dans leur modèle de la grammaire il y a une branche particulière, la lexicologie, dont le but est d'expliquer «tout ce qui concerne la connoissance des mots» (Grammaire, *E.M.*, tome II, p. 192), une définition grammaticale du mot semblerait une condition nécessaire et un fondement indispensable. Or, dans l'article «Mot», Beauzée se borne à préciser qu'il y a trois façons d'approcher le mot: en tant que porteur de sens, en tant que forme grammaticale, et en tant qu'élément historique dans l'évolution des langues: «Il y a trois choses à considérer dans les *Mots*; le matériel, l'étymologie, & la valeur» (Mot, *E.M.*, tome II, p. 570)[7]. Et l'abbé Féraud dans son *Dictionnaire grammatical*[8] sera encore plus sommaire, en se bornant à indiquer la prononciation: «MOT. *subst. masc.* prononcez *mot*, le *t* final s'y prononce toujours»!

1. Mais l'absence de progrès dans la définition, du point de vue linguistique, de la nature du mot, de Maupas aux Idéologues[9], ne doit pas faire oublier que l'approche descriptive du mot s'élargit, par l'intégration de l'étymologie, et que le fonctionnement du mot comme signe de la pensée est de plus en plus explicité.

En effet, si les Port-Royalistes envisagent le mot surtout au niveau de la *production* (perspective du locuteur) et de sa *constitution* (ensemble de sons distincts et articulés), la définition de Beauzée relève d'autres conditions indispensables au fonctionnement discursif du mot-signe:

[6] Cf. la Préface (par Claude Lancelot), p. 3-4: «L'ENGAGEMENT où je me suis trouvé, plustost par rencontre que par mon choix, de travailler aux Grammaires de diverses langues, m'a souvent porté à rechercher les raisons de plusieurs choses qui sont ou communes à toutes les langues, ou particulieres à quelques-unes. Mais y ayant quelquefois trouvé des difficultez qui m'arrestoient, je les ay communiquées dans les rencontres à un de mes Amis, qui ne s'estant jamais appliqué à cette sorte de science, n'a pas laissé de me donner beaucoup d'ouvertures pour resoudre mes doutes. Et mes questions mesme ont esté cause qu'il a fait diverses reflexions sur les vrays fondemẽs de l'Art de parler, dont m'ayant entretenu dans la conversation, je les trouvay si solides, que je fis conscience de les laisser perdre n'ayant rien veu dans les anciens Grammairiens, ny dans les nouveaux, qui fust plus curieux ou plus juste, sur cette matiere. C'est pourquoy j'obtins encore de la bonté qu'il a pour moy, qu'il me les dictast à des heures perduës; & ainsi les ayant recueillies & mises en ordre, j'en ay cõposé ce petit Traité».

[7] Cf. Swiggers (1984a: 39-60, 61-105), pour une analyse de cette approche multiple des mots chez les grammairiens de l'*Encyclopédie*.

[8] Voir Féraud (1788, vol. II, p. 128).

[9] Pour des bibliographies couvrant cette période, voir note 10; pour le XVIIIe siècle, voir Régaldo (1970), Aarsleff (1975;1979); Porset (1977), Dominicy (1979) et Swiggers (1983c).

(a) le mot doit être une expression linguistique «totale» ou complète, par exemple «*chapeau*». Mais si «*chapeau*» entre dans l'expression «*porte-chapeaux*», ce n'est plus une forme fonctionnant comme un mot. Dès lors, une seconde condition doit être posée:

(b) l'expression doit être celle d'une idée totale:

«Je dis qu'un *Mot* est le signe d'une idée totale; & il y a plusieurs raisons pour m'exprimer ainsi. La première, c'est qu'on ne peut pas disconvenir que souvent une seule syllabe ou même une simple articulation ne soit le signe d'une idée, puisqu'il n'y a ni inflexion ni terminaison qui n'ait sa signification propre: mais les objets de cette signification ne sont que des idées partielles, & le *Mot* entier est nécessaire à l'expression de l'idée totale. La seconde raison, c'est que, si l'on n'attachoit pas à la signification du *Mot* une idée totale, on pourroit dire que le *Mot* diversement terminé demeure le même, sous prétexte qu'il exprime toujours la même idée principale: mais l'idée principale & les idées accessoires sont également partielles, & le moindre changement qui arrive dans l'une ou dans l'autre est un changement réel pour la totalité; le *Mot* alors n'est plus le même, c'en est un autre, parce qu'il est le signe d'une autre idée totale. Une troisième raison, c'est que la notion du *Mot* ainsi entendue est vraie de ceux même qui équivalent à des propositions entières, comme *oui, non, allez, morieris*, etc.: car toute une proposition ne sert qu'à faire naître dans l'esprit de ceux qui l'entendent une idée plus précise & plus dèvelopée du sujet» (Mot, *E.M.*, tome II, p. 583).

(c) le mot doit avoir été établi *conventionnellement* comme le signe d'une idée:

«Ainsi c'est l'usage qui autorise les *Mots*, qui en détermine le sens & l'emploi, qui en est l'instituteur véritable & l'unique approbateur» (Mot, *E.M.*, tome II, p. 584).

(d) le mot doit être entendu (et compris): pas de signe sans récepteur.

Mais le progrès le plus important est que, en dépit de la stagnation de la définition grammaticale du mot, les classes de mots sont mieux dégagées et décrites. L'évolution qu'on observe — et qui sera retracée ci-après —, va dans le sens d'une classification morpho-syntaxique des classes de mots, définies de plus en plus en termes de catégories grammaticales et de valeur syntaxique, et moins en fonction de leur contenu sémantique.

2. Les grammaires françaises du XVIIe siècle — celles de Maupas, Oudin, Chiflet, Irson, Filz, de Foigny, Vairasse d'Allais[10] — sont

[10] Pour une bibliographie, voir Stengel (1890), Stengel - Niederehe (1976; cf. Wüest 1978; Swiggers 1979), Mertens (1968), Slatkine (1971), Swiggers - Mertens (1984). Pour des études consacrées à des auteurs particuliers, voir Winkler (1912), Brunot (1909-1915; réédition 1966), Hanse (1962), Chevalier (1968: 420-589), Swiggers (1982a; 1984b; 1984c),

construites, comme celles du XVIe (Sylvius, Meigret, Estienne, Ramus, etc.), autour du schéma des parties du discours, qui comprend le nom (substantif et adjectif), le pronom, le verbe, l'adverbe, le participe (qui n'est pas considéré comme partie du discours par tous les auteurs), la préposition, la conjonction, l'interjection, et très souvent l'article[11]. Précédée le plus souvent d'une partie phonétique (et orthographique), la partie morphologique de ces grammaires définit le sens de chaque partie du discours — si une classe de mots est subdivisée, c'est en fonction d'un critère sémantique (cf. nom propre vs nom appellatif/commun; pronom possessif vs pronom démonstratif) —, et fournit une description des «accidents» de chaque partie du discours (par exemple: genre, nombre et cas pour le nom; mode, temps, voix, nombre et personne pour le verbe). La description concerne donc avant tout des caractéristiques morphologiques[12], même si celles-ci ont une incidence syntaxique (par exemple l'emploi des temps, des modes ...). C'est la réflexion sur cette incidence syntaxique qui conduira à un embryon de syntaxe, centrée sur les phénomènes d'accord et de rection[13], dans les grammaires de la

Scheemaeker (1983), Missinne (1984), Stéfanini (1984). Sur Vaugelas, voir maintenant Marzys (1984).

[11] Sur l'histoire, très complexe, de l'article dans la grammatographie française, voir Swiggers (1985a).

[12] Cf. aussi la distinction entre formes simples et composées (ou dérivées).

[13] Cf. la *Grammaire* de Port-Royal (1660), où Lancelot et Arnauld distinguent entre une syntaxe de convenance et une syntaxe de régime. La syntaxe de convenance est la même dans toutes les langues, parce que «c'est une suitte naturelle de ce qui est en usage presque partout» (*Grammaire* II, 23, p. 140). À cette syntaxe de convenance appartiennent la concordance en genre et en nombre entre le substantif et l'adjectif qui l'accompagne, et la concordance en nombre et en personne entre les verbes et les noms ou pronoms (sujets). La syntaxe de régime diffère d'une langue à l'autre: l'exemple que la *Grammaire* donne est celui de l'expression des relations syntaxiques. Celles-ci sont exprimées dans certaines langues à l'aide de flexions casuelles, d'autres langues emploient des particules et des prépositions; finalement il y a des langues qui n'emploient aucun morphème lexical ou grammatical pour exprimer les relations syntaxiques, l'ordre des mots servant à les rendre. Ensuite, les auteurs formulent quelques règles générales en rapport avec la syntaxe. Ils font remarquer que

1. tout nominatif suppose un verbe (qui parfois n'est pas exprimé);
2. tout verbe suppose un nominatif (qui parfois n'est pas exprimé);
3. tout adjectif suppose un substantif (qui parfois n'est pas exprimé);
4. tout génitif suppose un substantif qu'il détermine;
5. la même relation, avec des verbes différents, peut être exprimée par des cas différents ou par des prépositions différentes. Ceci est dû à l'élément non rationnel dans la langue: «le caprice de l'usage».

Ces deux types de syntaxe constituent la syntaxe naturelle, qui se distingue de la syntaxe non naturelle, qui englobe les figures de construction (syllepse, ellipse, pléonasme); cf. Donzé (1967: 159-171). Chez Oudin (1632) et Chiflet (1659), la syntaxe n'est guère seconde moitié du XVIIe siècle. Dans celles de la première moitié du XVIIe siècle, par contre, la syntaxe est intégrée à la morphologie, et n'a qu'une portée restreinte (emploi des temps et des modes, régime des verbes, compléments déterminatifs).

Dans ce contexte, la *Grammaire* de Port-Royal occupe une place à part. Tout en continuant la tradition, elle systématise le schéma des parties du discours en le rapportant à une théorie des opérations mentales. Les opérations de l'esprit, envisagées du point de vue de l'analyse dialectique — et basées sur les principes de la rhétorique renaissanciste[14] —, sont situées à trois niveaux: le *concevoir*, le *juger* et le *raisonner*. Le niveau du concevoir concerne l'appréhension et l'expression des choses, «soit d'une maniere purement intellectuelle; comme quand je connois l'estre, la durée, la pensée, Dieu: soit avec des images corporelles, comme quand je m'imagine un quarré, un rond, un chien, un cheval» (*Grammaire* II, 1, p. 27-28; *Logique*, vol. I, p. 23-24). Juger, c'est utiliser des termes construits au niveau précédent, et affirmer une relation d'identité ou de non-identité entre eux. Le raisonnement est la déduction[15] d'un jugement à partir d'un enchaînement de jugements (cf. syllogisme, sorite).

Les classes de mots peuvent être regroupées en deux ensembles, selon qu'elles se rapportent au concevoir ou au juger.

développée. Vairasse d'Allais consacre plus de soixante pages à la syntaxe (1681: 435-498), dont le rôle est de traiter de «l'assemblage ou arrangement artificiel des diverses parties du discours, pour la composition reguliere des Sentences, des Phrases, & des Periodes, selon le genie & la constitution de chaque Langue» (p. 435). La syntaxe comprend deux branches chez lui: la *construction* (ou arrangement) des mots et le *régime*. Par construction, Vairasse entend l'ordre respectif des mots (place des articles, pronoms, adjectifs, participes, etc.; l'ordre des mots dans les phrases affirmatives, négatives et interrogatives). Dans l'étude du régime, Vairasse considère la concordance de l'adjectif, de l'article, du pronom (possessif, démonstratif, ...) ou du participe avec le nom substantif qu'ils accompagnent (p. 468-478), la concordance du nominatif avec le verbe (p. 480-481), la valence verbale (p. 481-485), le régime des modes (p. 485-490), le régime de l'infinitif (p. 490-493), et le régime de quelques «Noms adjectifs, & des Noms matériels» (p. 493-496).

[14] Cf. les études de Ong (1958), Nuchelmans (1980) et Webster (1984).

[15] C'est la conception (trop étroite) qu'ont les Port-Royalistes du raisonnement: «RAISONNER, est se servir de deux jugemens pour en faire un troisiéme. Comme lors qu'ayant jugé que toute vertu est loüable, & que la patience est une vertu, j'en conclus que la patience est loüable. D'où l'on voit que la troisiéme operation de l'esprit, n'est qu'une extension de la seconde. Et ainsi il suffira pour nostre sujet de considerer les deux premieres, ou ce qui est enfermé de la premiere dans la seconde. Car les hommes ne parlent gueres pour exprimer simplement ce qu'ils conçoivent; mais c'est presque tousiours pour exprimer les jugemens qu'ils font des choses qu'ils conçoivent» (*Grammaire* II, 1, p. 27-28; *Logique*, vol. I, p. 23-24).

«Et ainsi la plus grande distinction de ce qui se passe dans nostre esprit, est de dire qu'on y peut considerer l'objet de nostre pensée; & la forme ou la maniere de nôtre pensée, dont la principale est le jugement. Mais on y doit encore rapporter les conjonctions, disjonctions, & autres semblables operations de nostre esprit; & tous les autres mouvemens de nostre ame; comme les desirs, le commandement, l'interrogation, &c. Il s'ensuit de là que les hommes ayant eu besoin de signes pour marquer tout ce qui se passe dans leur esprit, il faut aussi la plus generale distinction des mots, soit que les uns signifient les objets des pensées, & les autres la forme & la maniere de nos pensées, quoy que souvent ils ne la signifient pas seule, mais avec l'objet, comme nous le ferons voir. Les mots de la première sorte sont ceux qu'on a appellez *noms, articles, pronoms, participes, prepositions, & adverbes.* Ceux de la seconde, sont *les verbes, les conjonctions, & les interjections.* Qui sont tous tirez par une suitte necessaire de la maniere naturelle en laquelle nous exprimons nos pensées, comme nous l'allons monstrer» (*Grammaire* II, 1, p. 29-30).

On peut se demander pourquoi les auteurs de la *Grammaire* rangent l'article, la préposition et l'adverbe dans la catégorie des mots qui signifient les «objets» de notre pensée[16]. En effet, ces mots ne peuvent fonctionner comme sujet dans un jugement (ce qu'on devrait normalement attendre des mots qui signifient les objets de notre pensée). Duclos avait déjà relevé ce problème:

«MESSIEURS de P.R. établissent dans ce chapitre les vrais fondements sur lesquels portent (*sic*) la métaphysique des langues. Tous les grammairiens qui s'en sont écartés ou qui ont voulu les déguiser, sont tombés dans l'erreur ou dans l'obscurité. M. du Marsais, en adoptant le principe de P.R., a eu raison d'en rectifier l'application au sujet des vues de l'esprit. En effet, MM. de P.R., après avoir si bien distingué les mots qui signifient les objets des pensées, d'avec ceux qui marquent la manière de nos pensées, ne devaient pas mettre dans la première classe, l'article, la préposition, ni même l'adverbe. L'article et la préposition appartiennent à la seconde; et l'adverbe, contenant une préposition et un nom, pourrait, sous différents aspects, se rappeler à l'une et à l'autre classe»[17].

Quant à l'article, on pourrait proposer l'explication suivante: comme en français classique (et moderne), le substantif est (presque) toujours accompagné d'un article qui (co-)détermine l'extension de l'idée signifiée par le substantif, on peut considérer l'article, en tant que membre du groupe nominal, comme un élément qui contribue à l'expression d'un concept (déterminé ou indéterminé). Dans le cas de la préposition, on peut faire valoir que jointe à un ou à deux substantifs (ou pronoms) elle désigne la relation conçue entre deux choses, deux personnes, etc. (*la maison du roi*; *il est chez le roi*). Les adverbes sont considérés comme des

[16] Voir la discussion de ce problème chez Dominicy (1977; 1984: 149-151).

[17] Pour les éditions du texte de Duclos, voir Swiggers - Mertens (1983: 358-360).

mots qui signifient les objets de notre pensée, parce qu'ils sont une forme elliptique d'une construction plus complexe (préposition + substantif), dont les éléments constitutifs appartiennent chacun à la classe des mots qui signifient les objets de notre pensée:

«Le desir que les hommes ont d'abreger le discours, est ce qui a donné lieu aux Adverbes. Car la pluspart de ces particules ne sont que pour signifier en un seul mot, ce qu'on ne pourroit marquer que par une preposition & un nom: comme *sapienter*, sagement, pour *cum sapientia*, avec sagesse» (*Grammaire* II, chapitre XI — d'après la numérotation incorrecte de la première édition —, p. 88).

Cette dichotomie, à base fonctionnelle, semble être un avatar de la distinction médiévale entre *categoremata* et *syncategoremata*: les premiers sont les termes (le plus souvent à base nominale) qui fonctionnent de façon autonome dans le discours. On tiendra compte ici du fait que l'article, inexistant en latin classique, n'est pas mentionné par les grammairiens médiévaux, et que la perspective est celle d'une priorité du sujet (nominal) à l'égard du prédicat (verbal). C'est donc à partir des *categoremata* (nom, pronom, participe) que les relations proportionnelles se nouent dans une phrase. Les termes syncatégorématiques sont donc ceux qui combinent deux ou plusieurs catégorèmes, ou qui énoncent une action, un état, une qualité d'un élément exprimé sous forme de catégorème.

Reste que la position des Port-Royalistes diffère sensiblement de celle des grammairiens du moyen âge: la classe des *categoremata* semble avoir fait place à une classe d'éléments nominaux (ou leurs équivalents), adnominaux (l'article et la préposition), ou à base nominale (les adverbes). Ce point de vue, justifiable dans une certaine mesure, se heurte à quelques problèmes de taille: le statut du participe (qu'on pense aux propositions participiales), la présence très nette d'éléments nominaux dans les interjections, les limites fluctuantes entre les prépositions et les conjonctions (*avant, avant que*). On s'attendrait ici à voir appuyée la dichotomie objet/forme sur des arguments syntaxiques.

Il importe maintenant d'analyser la description des différentes classes de mots chez les Port-Royalistes. Nous respecterons leur division en termes désignant les objets de la pensée (2.1.1. à 2.1.6.) et en termes désignant la forme de notre pensée (2.2.1. à 2.2.2.).

2.1.1. *Les substantifs et les adjectifs*

Notre pensée se rapporte à la réalité extérieure et avant de pouvoir juger de la réalité (ou non-réalité) d'une chose, il faut la concevoir:

«CONCEVOIR, n'est autre chose qu'un simple regard de nostre esprit sur les choses, soit d'une maniere purement intellectuelle; comme quand je connois l'estre, la durée, la pensée, Dieu: soit avec des images corporelles, comme quand je m'imagine un quarré, un rond, un chien, un cheval» (*Grammaire* II, 1, p. 27-28).

Notre pensée n'est pas pour autant une imitation servile de la réalité. Les Port-Royalistes insistent sur ce point lorsqu'ils traitent des substantifs. D'après la *Grammaire*, une première distinction à l'intérieur de la classe des substantifs a son fondement dans la réalité même:

«Les objets de nos pensées, sont ou les choses, comme *la terre, le Soleil, l'eau, le bois*, ce qu'on appelle ordinairement *substance*. Ou la maniere des choses; comme d'estre *rond*, d'estre *rouge*, d'estre *dur*, d'estre *sçavant*, &c., ce qu'on appelle *accident*. Et il y a cette difference entre les choses ou les substances, & la maniere des choses ou les accidens; que les substances subsistent par elles-mesmes, au lieu que les accidens ne sont que par les substances» (*Grammaire* II, 2, p. 30-31).

Les substances sont signifiées par les substantifs, les accidents par les adjectifs (*Grammaire* II, 2, p. 31). Jusqu'à ce point, notre pensée reflète la structure de la réalité, divisée en substances et en accidents. «Mais on n'en est pas demeuré-là. & il se trouve qu'on ne s'est pas tant arresté à la signification, qu'à la maniere de signifier» (*Grammaire* II, 2, p. 31). Il faut en effet tenir compte du caractère connotatif des mots: si un mot est employé connotativement, il renvoie «de façon confuse» à une substance qui porte les accidents[18]. On a donc trois types de substantifs: (A_1) le type qui correspond à l'idée d'une substance en tant que substance («*homme*»); (A_2) le type qui correspond à l'idée des accidents non connotatifs («*dureté*»); (A_3) le type qui correspond à l'idée des substances abstraites («*humanité*»). Pour les adjectifs, deux types sont à distinguer: (B_1) le type qui correspond à l'idée d'un accident en tant qu'accident («*dur*») et (B_2) le type correspondant à l'idée des substances connotatives («*humain*»). On voit donc que A_2 est une abstraction de B_1,

[18] *Grammaire* II, 2, p. 31-32: «Or ce qui fait qu'un nom ne peut subsister par soy-mesme; est quand outre sa signification distincte; il y en a encore une confuse, qu'on peut appeller connotation d'une chose, à laquelle convient ce qui est marqué par la signification distincte. Ainsi la signification distincte de *rouge*, est la *rougeur*. Mais il la signifie, en marquant confusément le sujet de cette rougeur, d'où vient qu'il ne subsiste point seul dans le discours, parce qu'on y doit exprimer ou sous-entendre le mot qui signifie ce sujet». Chez les Port-Royalistes, la connotation concerne l'emploi discursif des mots et la relation avec l'objet signifié, alors que le terme «signification distincte» renvoie à la signification purement lexicographique d'un mot en dehors de tout contexte discursif. Voir, à propos de la connotation, Padley (1976: 245-248). Sur la théorie du substantif et de l'adjectif (et son rapport avec la connotation) chez les Port-Royalistes, voir Murat (1979) et Swiggers (1981a).

que B_2 est égal à A_1 rendu connotatif et que A_3 est une abstraction de B_2. Dans l'optique des auteurs de la *Grammaire*, les substantifs sont donc des mots non connotatifs, alors que les adjectifs sont toujours connotatifs: ils signifient l'accident et le support de l'accident. Les mots connotatifs ont donc une *référence directe* (renvoi à la substance connotée) et une *référence indirecte* (la «signification distincte» du terme même).

«Ainsi *blanc, candidus*, signifie directement ce qui a de la blancheur; *habens candorem*; mais d'une maniere fort confuse, ne marquant en particulier aucune des choses qui peuvent avoir de la blancheur & il ne signifie qu'indirectement la blancheur; mais d'une maniere aussi distincte que le mot mesme de blancheur, *candor*» (*Grammaire*, II, 2, p. 34).

Les substantifs peuvent être divisés d'après ce qu'on peut appeler la «charge extensionnelle» de l'idée (ou du concept) dont ils sont le signe. S'il s'agit de l'idée d'un individu en tant qu'individu, nous avons à faire à un nom propre; s'il s'agit de l'idée d'une classe (espèce ou genre), nous avons à faire à un nom général (ou «nom appellatif» ou encore «nom commun»; *Grammaire* II, 3, p. 35). Les auteurs de la *Grammaire* semblent perdre de vue ici que cette distinction ne s'applique qu'aux substantifs du type A_1 (les substantifs du type A_2 ou A_3 signifient toujours soit une espèce soit un genre).

Ensuite, il est question des morphèmes flexionnels des substantifs qui marquent le nombre, le genre ou le cas. Le nombre est une catégorie flexionnelle qui s'applique aux noms communs et à tous les adjectifs, car «il est de leur nature d'enfermer tousiours une certaine signification vague d'un sujet, qui fait qu'ils peuvent convenir à plusieurs, au moins quant à la maniere de signifier, quoy qu'en effet ils ne convinssent qu'à un» (*Grammaire*, II, 4, p. 38). Le genre est une catégorie grammaticale qui appartient au nom substantif et au nom adjectif. Originellement, le genre appartient, en tant que catégorie flexionnelle, aux adjectifs: «Comme les noms adjectifs de leur nature conviennent à plusieurs, on a jugé à propos pour rendre le discours moins confus, & aussi pour l'embellir par la varieté des terminaisons, d'inventer dans les adjectifs une diversité selon les substantifs ausquels on les appliqueroit» (*Grammaire* II, 5, p. 39). La variation en genre de l'adjectif a un fondement ontologique:

«Or les hommes se sont premierement considerez eux-mesmes, & ayant remarqué parmy eux une difference extrémement considerable, qui est celle des deux sexes, ils ont jugé à propos de varier les mesmes noms adjectifs (...) Et c'est ce qu'ils ont appellé *genre masculin & feminin*» (*Grammaire* II, 5, p. 39).

Une conséquence de cette vue théorique est que les auteurs de la *Grammaire* doivent admettre, *post dictum*, des substantifs masculins et féminins. Cette distinction peut être motivée ontologiquement, mais il reste des exceptions (cf. *Grammaire* II, 5, p. 40). En ce qui concerne le neutre, les Port-Royalistes font remarquer que ce genre aurait dû regrouper des substantifs qui sont «neutres» par rapport au genre masculin et au genre féminin. Mais les langues n'ont pas toujours suivi cette règle logique ... Un point important ici est que les Port-Royalistes considèrent le genre comme une caractéristique originelle des adjectifs, qui peuvent connoter des personnes ou des animaux masculins ou féminins (désignés par des substantifs). Le genre des substantifs n'est donc pas, d'après les auteurs de la *Grammaire*, une catégorie grammaticale de base: en effet, ils considèrent que le genre du substantif est le même que le sexe de la personne (ou de l'animal) à laquelle le substantif renvoie et qu'il ne doit donc pas être marqué par un élément (morphème) grammatical[19].

Ensuite, les auteurs discutent les cas du nom: ceux-ci signifient les relations conçues entre les choses. On peut donc inférer que la flexion casuelle est une propriété originelle des substantifs, le morphème flexionnel renvoyant ici aux relations conçues entre les choses (cf. *Grammaire* II, 6, p. 44-51 pour les différents types de relations). Par analogie, les adjectifs auraient adopté cette propriété.

2.1.2. *Les articles*

Les chapitres sur les noms substantifs et adjectifs sont suivis par un chapitre sur l'article. Les articles, caractérisés par les catégories du genre, du nombre et du cas, servent à co-déterminer la signification des noms communs (et dans certaines langues, comme le grec et l'italien, celle des noms propres aussi). Pour étudier cette co-détermination, les auteurs proposent une analyse des concepts tels qu'ils apparaissent dans les jugements (*Grammaire* II, 7, p. 56). Cette analyse contient en germe toute la théorie de la détermination qu'on trouvera dans les grammaires jusqu'au XXe siècle: (1) typologie basée sur l'emploi ou l'absence d'un article; (2) distinction entre la série *le, la, les*, et la série *un, une, des*; (3) description du sémantisme (à partir des effets de sens) de ces structures. Voici le tableau qu'on trouve dans la *Grammaire* de Port-Royal:

[19] *Grammaire* II, 5 et II, 6, p. 43: «Si l'on consideroit tousiours les choses separément les unes des autres, on n'auroit donné aux noms que les deux changemens que nous venons de marquer, sçavoir du nombre pour toute sorte de noms, & du genre pour les adjectifs».

Le nom commun, comme ROI

Sans article,	ou n'a qu'une signification fort confuse:	Il a fait un festin de roi. Ils ont fait des festins de rois.
	ou en a une déterminée par le sujet de la proposition:	Louis XIV est roi. Louis XIV et Philippe IV sont rois.
Avec l'article *le*, signifie ou	L'espèce dans toute son étendue:	Le roi ne dépend point de ses sujets. Les rois ne dépendent point de leurs sujets.
	Un ou plusieurs singuliers déterminés par les circonstances de celui qui parle, ou du discours:	Le roi fait la paix: c'est-à-dire le roi Louis XIV, à cause des circonstances du temps. Les rois ont fondé les principales abbayes de France; c'est-à-dire les rois de France.

Avec l'article	*Un* au singulier, *des* ou *de* au pluriel,	signifie	un *ou* plusieurs	individus vagues:	Un roi détruira Constantinople. Rome a été gouvernée par des rois (ou) par de grands rois.

Comme le note André Joly (1980: 23-24), «Arnauld et Lancelot mettent bien en valeur les conditions discursives de la détermination en distinguant ce que nous appelons la détermination contextuelle, celle qui résulte des «circonstances du discours» (*Les rois ont fondé les principales abbayes de France*) et la détermination situationnelle produite par «les circonstances de celui qui parle» (*Le roi fait la paix*). Dans ce dernier cas, *le roi* constitue ce qu'Arnauld et Nicole nommeront dans la *Logique* un terme complexe dans le sens». Reste que l'analyse des Port-Royalistes est insatisfaisante sur plus d'un point: non seulement la notion de «détermination» n'est pas expliquée, mais les valeurs dégagées à partir d'une analyse conceptuelle (compréhension/extension) ne sont pas reliées à des valeurs grammaticales (nom commun vs nom propre; emploi d'un nom dans un syntagme déterminatif; le statut des déterminants devant des noms suivis d'une relative), ni à des valeurs pragma-sémantiques (type d'énoncé: vérité générale, description d'un état de choses, etc.).

2.1.3. *Les pronoms*

Lancelot et Arnauld considèrent les pronoms comme une classe secondaire:

«Comme les hommes ont esté obligez de parler souvent des mesmes choses dans mesme discours, & qu'il eust esté importun de repeter tousiours les mesmes noms, ils ont inventé certains mots pour tenir la place de ces noms, & que pour cette raison ils ont appellé *Pronoms*» (*Grammaire* II, 8, p. 59).

En tant que substituts des noms substantifs, les pronoms sont caractérisés par les mêmes traits formels: nombre, genre, cas. Les pronoms renvoient à des substances, conçues en tant que telles. Les pronoms possessifs constituent pourtant une exception: ceux-ci appartiennent en effet à la classe des adjectifs dérivés des substantifs. On a donc, pour le pronom de la première personne du singulier:

A Substantif	B Adjectif
1. «*je*»	1. —
	2. «*mon*», «*ma*», ...

Les pronoms possessifs ont comme signification distincte le (sujet) possesseur, signifié indirectement, et comme signification confuse l'objet possédé, signifié directement (*Grammaire* II, 8, p. 65; *Logique* II, 1, vol. 2, p. 93-94).

Le pronom relatif reçoit un traitement détaillé (*Grammaire* II, 9 et II, 10[20]). Si le pronom relatif a quelques caractéristiques en commun avec les autres pronoms, il possède aussi quelques traits particuliers. Le trait le plus typique du pronom relatif est qu'il accompagne un substantif ou un pronom personnel et qu'il réunit deux propositions en une phrase. Le pronom relatif se joint toujours au sujet (ou à une partie du sujet) ou au prédicat (ou à une partie du prédicat), mais jamais à la copule.

S (+ pronom relatif) copule P (+ pronom relatif)[21]

[20] Ce dernier chapitre est numéroté, par erreur, IX; notre numération à l'aide de chiffres arabes renvoie aux chapitres de chaque partie dénombrés successivement.

[21] Les parenthèses indiquent des relations facultatives. Comme phrases-exemples de pronoms relatifs se joignant au sujet ou à une partie du sujet, on peut mentionner: *Jean, qui était malade, ne pouvait venir* et *Le fils du colonel qui habite en face de nous est mort*. Des exemples de pronoms relatifs se joignant au prédicat et à une partie du prédicat sont: *Jean est le patron qu'il nous faut* et *Jean est le prototype du patron qu'il nous faut*. Dans la *Grammaire* II, 9, p. 68-69 on trouve l'analyse de la phrase célèbre *Dieu invisible a créé le*

La proposition introduite par le pronom relatif n'est qu'une composante (d'une partie) du sujet ou du prédicat de la principale et ne constitue jamais à elle seule le sujet ou le prédicat de la principale (*Grammaire* II, 9, p. 70-71).

2.1.4. *Les participes*

Formes adjectivales du verbe, les participes conservent la distinction actif/passif (*Grammaire* II, 21, p. 131-133), et l'indication du temps[22]; mais ils n'expriment pas une affirmation, comme le fait le verbe conjugué. De ce fait, les participes ne peuvent être considérés comme des termes exprimant la forme de notre pensée. Leur signification est celle d'un objet conçu par l'esprit.

2.1.5. *Les prépositions*

Selon Arnauld et Lancelot, les prépositions constituent en quelque sorte une catégorie redondante: une langue complètement «synthétique» exprimerait les rapports entre les idées par des variations flexionnelles dans les substantifs et les adjectifs. Mais une telle langue n'existe pas: on trouve toujours, parfois à côté des marques casuelles, des prépositions qui ont la même fonction. Ce qu'on peut faire, d'après les Port-Royalistes, c'est établir un schéma «universel» (basé sur les prépositions qui existent en français!) des rapports qui peuvent être exprimés par les prépositions (*Grammaire* II, 11, p. 84). Ces rapports sont considérés par les Port-Royalistes comme des objets de la pensée.

2.1.6. *Les adverbes*

Les adverbes constituent une classe doublement secondaire: l'adverbe (par exemple *sapienter*) est secondaire par rapport à la construction «préposition + substantif» (*cum sapientiā*), elle-même secondaire par rapport au substantif décliné à un certain cas (l'ablatif en latin: *sapientiā*).

monde visible (décomposée en trois jugements). Chomsky (1966: 31-51, surtout 33-35) y a reconnu une analyse (proto-)générative de la structure profonde des phrases; cette interprétation a été contestée par Zimmer (1968: 295-300), Hall (1969: 226-227), Uitti (1969: 78-79) et Kretzmann (1975: 182-186). Sur la phrase relative (et les termes complexes) dans la *Grammaire* de Port-Royal, voir maintenant l'analyse pénétrante de Dominicy (1984: 179-225).

[22] Il y a en effet des participes du présent, du passé et du futur; cf. *Grammaire* II, 19, p. 121 (voir aussi Donzé 1967/1971²: 200, note 40).

2.2.1. *Les verbes*

L'acte de juger consiste à affirmer[23] le lien entre deux termes: le sujet et l'attribut. La fonction essentielle du verbe est d'établir ce lien.

«Et c'est proprement ce que c'est que le verbe, *un mot dont le principal usage est de signifier l'affirmation*» (*Grammaire* II, 13, p. 90; *Logique* II, 2, vol. 2, p. 97-98).

Pour exprimer l'affirmation, on emploie l'indicatif du verbe. En fait, il n'y a qu'une seule forme verbale qui se borne à affirmer le lien entre les deux termes de la proposition: c'est la troisième personne de l'indicatif présent du verbe *être* (*Grammaire* II, 13, p. 91; *Logique* II, 2, vol. 2, p. 98). Les autres formes verbales contiennent une information additionnelle sur la personne (*sum* = *ego sum*), sur un attribut particulier (*vivit* = *est vivens*) ou sur une époque temporelle (*coenasti* = *fuisti coenans*). Après avoir parcouru et critiqué quelques définitions courantes du verbe, les Port-Royalistes donnent une définition minimale du verbe:

«Il doit donc demeurer pour constant qu'à ne considerer simplement que ce qui est essentiel au Verbe, sa seule vraye definition est, *vox significans affirmationem; un mot qui signifie l'affirmation*» (*Grammaire* II, 13, p. 96; *Logique* II, 2, vol. 2, p. 101).

Les traits accidentels du verbe sont: la personne, le nombre et le temps. Pour les verbes adjectifs (*Grammaire* II, 18, p. 115-116), il faut y ajouter l'attribut qu'ils signifient, c'est-à-dire leur signification lexicale (*Grammaire* II, 2, vol. 2, p. 101). Les auteurs de la *Grammaire* font remarquer que le contenu sémantique affirmé peut être une affirmation: «*affirmo*» signifie «*j'affirme*», et cette idée est affirmée par l'énoncé, et plus particulièrement par la force illocutionnaire du verbe.

«Car quand je dis, *Petrus affirmat, affirmat* est la mesme chose que *est affirmans*: & alors *est* marque mon affirmation, ou le jugement que je fais touchant Pierre & *affirmans*, l'affirmation que je conçois, & que j'attribuë à Pierre. Le verbe *nego* au contraire contient une affirmation & une negation par la mesme raison» (*Grammaire* II, 13, p. 98; *Logique* II, 2, vol. 2, p. 101).

Tout verbe employé à l'indicatif et utilisé dans une principale marque

[23] *Grammaire* II, 13, p. 89 et *Logique* II, 1, vol. 2, p. 97-98. L'affirmation est la principale modalité de notre pensée: «Ainsi les hommes n'ont pas eü moins de besoin d'inventer des mots qui marquassent l'*affirmation*, qui est la principale maniere de nostre pensée, que d'en inventer qui marquassent les objets de nostre pensée» (*Grammaire* II, 13, p. 89-90).

donc la présence d'un jugement. On peut schématiser ceci de la façon suivante[24]:

Δ verbe à l'indicatif (S - Ra - P)

Donc: «affirmo» = Δ est (ego Ra affirmans)

Ce «*est*» ne peut être nié: dès qu'il y a jugement, le verbe principal marque l'affirmation positive d'un contenu propositionnel[25]. Le verbe *nego* contient ainsi l'affirmation du lien entre «*ego*» et «*negans*» (cette dernière forme exprime la négation lexicale contenue dans *neg-o*).

On a donc: «nego» = Δ est (ego Ra negans).

2.2.1.1. *Personne, nombre, genre*

Ensuite, les auteurs de la *Grammaire* discutent deux catégories flexionnelles du verbe: la personne et le nombre (*Grammaire* II, 14, p. 99-102). La première personne permet au locuteur de parler de lui-même, la seconde personne sert à nommer l'interlocuteur[26]. Ces personnes sont également marquées par les pronoms personnels, qui dans certaines langues (par exemple le latin et le grec) ne sont pas obligatoires (les personnes sont alors marquées par les désinences verbales). La troisième personne, qui peut renvoyer à des personnes et à des choses, est considérée comme la forme de base du verbe, exprimant essentiellement l'affirmation. Quand les désinences ne sont plus distinguées dans la prononciation, l'emploi de pronoms personnels devient nécessaire (*Grammaire* II, 14, p. 101-102).

Quant au nombre (singulier, pluriel et, parfois, duel), Lancelot et Arnauld renvoient à l'explication qu'ils ont donnée à propos du nombre des substantifs (cf. *Grammaire* II, 4, p. 36-39), et ajoutent que dans certaines langues orientales (l'hébreu et l'araméen), les désinences du verbe marquent non seulement le nombre et la personne, mais également le genre (*Grammaire* II, 14, p. 102).

[24] Nous utilisons Δ comme signe de l'affirmation effectuée. *Ra* marque la relation d'être, par laquelle le sujet (ou l'argument) est lié au prédicat (ou foncteur) à l'aide d'une forme de l'indicatif du verbe *être*.

[25] Cf. Chevalier (1968: 506-509); Swiggers (1981b). La présence inéluctable de l'affirmation (liée à la performativité de l'énonciation) semble avoir échappé à Braußе (1983: 255-257); voir par contre Brekle (1969), Durand (1977), Swiggers (1980), Pariente (1982) et Dominicy (1984: 161-164).

[26] À propos de la structure des relations de personne, voir Benveniste (1946) et Hagège (1982: 95-100).

2.2.1.2. *Les temps*

Les auteurs distinguent trois temps simples: le présent, le prétérit et le futur (*Grammaire* II, 15, p. 104-107). À côté de ces temps simples, il y a des temps composés, qui marquent les rapports entre les temps simples:
1. l'imparfait, qui marque le passé par rapport à un présent;
2. le plus-que-parfait, qui marque le passé par rapport à un passé;
3. le futur du passé, qui marque le futur par rapport à un passé[27].
Les Port-Royalistes ajoutent:

«On auroit pû de mesme adjouster encore un quatriéme temps composé, sçavoir celuy qui eust marqué l'avenir avec rapport au present; pour faire autant de futurs composez, que de preterits composez» (*Grammaire* II, 15, p. 106)[28].

2.2.1.3. *Les modes*

Il y a deux sortes d'affirmations: les affirmations simples et les affirmations conditionnées et modifiées. Les premières sont exprimées par l'indicatif, les deuxièmes par le subjonctif (*Grammaire* II, 16, p. 107-108).

À côté de l'affirmation, il existe une autre modalité de la pensée, à savoir l'expression de la volonté. Celle-ci peut revêtir plusieurs formes: le souhait (auquel correspond, au plan grammatical, le mode *optatif*), la concession (exprimée par le mode *concessif*), ou l'ordre (rendu par le mode *impératif*). Quant à l'*infinitif*, celui-ci peut avoir la valeur d'un verbe (par exemple *esse* dans *Scio malum esse fugiendum*) ou celle d'un substantif (par exemple «*l'être*»). L'infinitif dans son emploi verbal est comparé au pronom relatif: tous les deux servent à lier des propositions.

«Car *scio*, vaut seule une proposition, & si vous ajoûtiez, *malum est fugiendum*, ce seroit deux propositions séparées. Mais mettant *esse*, au lieu d'*est*, vous faites que la derniere proposition n'est plus que partie de la premiere, comme nous avons expliqué plus au long dans le ch. 9 du Relatif» (*Grammaire* II, 17, p. 112).

La description des catégories grammaticales du verbe s'élargit ainsi, à partir d'une définition sémantico-pragmatique du verbe (conjugué), en

[27] *Grammaire* II, 15, p. 106. Il s'agit plutôt d'un passé par rapport au futur: «Le troisiéme temps composé est celuy qui marque l'avenir avec rapport au passé, sçavoir le futur parfait, comme *coenavero, j'auray soupé*, par où je marque mon action de souper comme future en soy; & comme passée au regard d'une autre chose à venir, qui la doit suivre; comme, *quand j'auray soupé il entrera*».

[28] Théoriquement, d'autres combinaisons sont possibles: présent par rapport à un présent (ce qui donne comme résultat un «présent corrélatif»), futur par rapport à un futur («plus-que-futur»), présent par rapport à un passé («présent gnomique»), présent par rapport à un futur («présent hypothétique»), futur par rapport à un passé (le futur du passé).

une description du fonctionnement du verbe: si l'intégration de la syntaxe est déjà visible dans la discussion des catégories du nombre et de la personne (qui supposent un rapport du verbe à un autre élément de la phrase, ou à un élément extra-discursif), elle est très nette dans la théorie des temps composés et des affirmations conditionnées et modifiées. Et la classification des verbes adjectifs (en verbes actifs, passifs, et neutres), même si elle est formulée en termes sémantiques, confirme l'intrusion de la syntaxe dans la morphologie.

2.2.2. *Conjonctions et interjections*

Par «conjonctions», les auteurs de la *Grammaire* entendent non seulement des mots comme «*et*», «*vel*», «*si*» en latin, mais également des adverbes comme «*non*» et des particules comme «*ergo*». Ces mots ne marquent pas un objet de la pensée, mais ils expriment l'activité de notre esprit qui distingue, nie et réunit, ou bien ils expriment un mouvement d'âme.

«Par exemple, il n'y a point d'objet dans le monde hors de nostre esprit, qui réponde à la particule *non*, mais il est clair qu'elle ne marque autre chose que le jugement que nous faisons qu'une chose n'est pas une autre. De mesme *ne*, qui est en Latin la particule de l'interrogation, *aisne*? Dites-vous? n'a point d'objet hors de nostre esprit, mais marque seulement le mouvement de nostre ame, par lequel nous souhaittons de sçavoir une chose» (*Grammaire* II, 22, p. 138).

Il est remarquable que le pronom interrogatif soit considéré comme la combinaison d'un pronom (personnel) avec la signification de la particule interrogative:

«Et c'est ce qui fait que je n'ay point parlé du Pronom interrogatif, *quis, quae, quid*: parce que ce n'est autre chose qu'un pronom, auquel est jointe la signification de *ne*» (*Grammaire* II, 22, p. 138).

Quant aux interjections, celles-ci ne signifient pas des contenus mentaux, mais elles marquent nos sentiments et nos états d'âme (*Grammaire* II, 22, p. 140).

3. La *Grammaire* de Port-Royal, en subordonnant les données morphologiques et syntaxiques à un schéma logico-sémantique, ne pouvait élaborer une classification grammaticale des espèces de mots. Après Lancelot et Arnauld, on assiste à un va-et-vient entre l'approche sémantique et l'approche formaliste. Ainsi, Vairasse d'Allais, dans sa *Grammaire méthodique*, semble se concentrer sur les propriétés formelles des classes de mots, en traitant tous leurs accidents ou «circonstances».

C'est ainsi que sa description du nom comprend les sections suivantes[29]: l'espèce, la figure, le genre, le nombre, les cas, la déclinaison, et la comparaison. Mais sous la déclinaison l'auteur traite de la détermination du nom, dont il fournit une description originale, mais nettement sémantique. Détermination et indétermination ne dépendent pas de la forme des articles, mais de la «signification des termes ausquels ils sont attachez» (p. 91). Et pour expliquer l'article partitif, l'auteur recourt à une distinction entre noms *dividuels* («dont on se sert pour representer les matieres divisibles»; *du vin/du pain*), et noms *individuels* (désignant les «substances bornées par la forme ou la figure, & qui tombent dans l'idée du nombre», p. 101-103). Vairasse d'Allais marque ainsi un retour, peu hardi pour le reste, à la tradition latinisante, axée sur les données morphologiques. Ce retour est encore plus nettement marqué dans la grammaire de Régnier-Desmarais (1705)[30] et dans celle de Restaut (1730)[31]. Par contre, la *Grammaire françoise* de Buffier (1709)[32] occupe une position originale dans l'histoire de la grammaire française au XVIIIe siècle. Partant du constat que la grammaire est loin d'être parfaite et souffre d'une certaine confusion dans ses définitions, Buffier s'efforce de proposer un systéme pour l'apprentissage de la grammaire et la rédaction de manuels grammaticaux. Il fait remarquer que la *Grammaire* de Port-Royal avait déjà proposé un système analogue, mais ces principes «n'ont point été appliqués à la pratique comme j'y applique ceux que je tâcherai d'établir» (§ 8). Pour l'établissement de son système de principes, il prend la voie opposée à celle des Port-Royalistes: alors que dans la *Grammaire* de Port-Royal la logique constitue le fondement explicatif des phénomènes grammaticaux et que l'usage y est censé s'ajuster aux lois de la pensée, Buffier affirme que «c'est essentiellement à la grammaire de s'ajuster aux langues pour lesquelles elle est faite, et dont elle n'est pour ainsi dire que le témoin, ou l'analyse» (§ 9 et § 25). Cette démarche empirique — qui maintient pourtant le lien entre pensée et parole — explique sans doute pourquoi les classes de mots ne sont pas des ensembles figés, mais des groupements d'entités mouvantes. Leur

[29] Voir aussi la description du pronom (p. 129-177), du verbe (p. 178-378), de l'adverbe (p. 378-391), et de la conjonction (p. 412-418), où chaque accident de ces classes de mots est discuté.

[30] Sur la grammaire de Régnier-Desmarais, voir Chevalier (1968: 590-598) et Vandekerckhove (1984).

[31] Sur cette grammaire, voir Chevalier (1968: 635-649), Mariën (1982) et Swiggers (1985b).

[32] Voir à ce propos: Chevalier (1968: 602-615), Aerts (1981) et Swiggers (1983b).

fonction (et, corrélativement, leur appartenance paradigmatique) ne peut être déterminée que par l'analyse syntagmatique. C'est sur ce point que Buffier apparaît comme un innovateur; dans l'analyse de la phrase il pose quatre notions: le *nom* (sujet thématique), le *verbe* (= le prédicat), le *modificatif* (comprenant l'adverbe, la préposition et la conjonction)[33], et le *terme de supplément* (impératifs des verbes, interjections, interrogatifs, *oui/non*, et les verbes impersonnels). Buffier, qui s'en tient à une définition très vague du mot[34], montre ainsi la relativité de la distinction en parties du discours. Les noms, verbes, modificatifs et termes de supplément ne correspondent pas chacun à une classe morphologique particulière: le substantif peut avoir la fonction de nom ou de modificatif dans la phrase, la forme verbale peut fonctionner comme nom (*aimer est un sentiment*), comme modificatif (*il continuait à parler sans se soucier de l'heure*), comme terme de supplément (impératif/verbe impersonnel) et fonctionnera le plus souvent comme verbe-prédicat. À la différence de la tradition latinisante, Buffier insiste sur l'aspect mouvant des parties du discours: un mot n'appartient pas forcément à une seule partie du discours. «Certains mots sont *adverbes, prépositions* et *conjonctions* en même temps: comme *après*; *il vint après*, il est là adverbe; *après vous*, il est là préposition; *après que j'eus parlé*, il est là conjonction. Certains mots répondent ainsi en même temps à diverses parties d'oraison, selon que la grammaire les emploie diversement» (§ 150).

Cette approche «par l'usage» (emploi syntaxique des «classes» de mots) ne connaîtra pas un grand succès au XVIIIe siècle (ni plus tard): les grammairiens favorisent l'idée de la fixité des classes de mots, soit en se fondant sur des caractéristiques morphologiques (Régnier-Desmarais, Restaut), soit en les considérant d'un point de vue sémantique ou sémasiologique (Girard, Condillac, Domergue). Même Silvestre de Sacy, riche de son expérience comme orientaliste, s'en tient à 10 «espèces de mots» (comprenant une classe d'articles et de «numératifs»).

Mais tous les auteurs de la seconde moitié du XVIIIe siècle sont redevables à Beauzée (article «Mot» dans l'*Encyclopédie*) d'une classification fortement hiérarchisée des parties du discours, où des critères sémiotiques, morphologiques et sémantiques sont dûment intégrés. C'est cette classification que nous allons considérer de plus près.

[33] Buffier fait remarquer que les adjectifs sont en fait des modificatifs du nom (même s'ils signifient, tout comme les substantifs, des objets de la pensée).

[34] «L'expression la plus simple dont on se serve par la parole, pour indiquer ses pensées» (§ 64).

4. Afin de ranger les mots en classes, Beauzée introduit d'abord un critère sémiotique: «à quel type d'*unité extralinguistique* le mot correspond-il?». Ce critère permet de distinguer les mots *affectifs* (les interjections), qui sont les signes naturels d'un sentiment, et les mots *énonciatifs*, signes arbitraires d'une idée.

«Or le premier coup d'œil jeté sur les langues montre sensiblement que le cœur & l'esprit ont chacun leur langage. Celui du cœur est inspiré par la nature, & n'a presque rien d'arbitraire: aussi est-il également entendu chez toutes les nations, & il semble même que les brutes qui nous environnent en ayent quelquefois l'intelligence; le vocabulaire en est court, il se réduit aux seules interjections, qui ont partout les mêmes radicaux, parce qu'elles tiennent à la constitution physique de l'organe (...) Elles désignent, dans celui qui s'en sert, une affection, un sentiment; elles ne l'excitent pas dans l'âme de celui qui les entend, elles ne lui en présentent que l'idée (...) Je donnerois à ce premier ordre de *Mots* le nom d'*affectifs*, pour le distinguer de ceux qui appartiennent au langage de l'esprit, & que je désignerois par le titre d'*énonciatifs*. Ceux-ci sont en plus grand nombre, ne sont que peu ou point naturels, & doivent leur existence & leur signification à la convention usuelle & fortuite de chaque nation» (Mot, *E.M.*, tome II, p. 571).

«Il y a donc en effet des parties d'oraison de deux espèces: les premières sont les signes naturels des sentiments; les autres sont les signes arbitraires des idées: celles-là constituent le langage du cœur, elles sont affectives; celles-ci appartiennent au langage de l'esprit, elles sont discursives. Je mets au premier rang les expressions du sentiment, parce qu'elles sont de première nécessité, les besoins du cœur étant antérieurs & supérieurs à ceux de l'esprit: d'ailleurs elles sont l'ouvrage de la nature, & les signes des idées sont de l'institution de l'art; ce qui est un second titre de prééminence, fondé sur celle de la nature même à l'égard de l'art» (Interjection, *E.M.*, tome II, p. 344).

Cette dichotomie fondamentale entre deux espèces de parties d'oraison est confirmée au niveau syntaxique: les interjections équivalent toujours à une proposition complexe (faisant «un sens total»), alors que les autres parties du discours ne constituent une proposition que s'il y a ellipse (par exemple dans une réponse à une question), ou dans le discours métalinguistique, ou quand ils intègrent un morphème indiquant le sujet et un morphème signifiant le prédicat (le verbe, ou un élément nominal à flexion ou tonalité verbale dans les langues «PRO-drop»: latin, hongrois, langues bantoues, ...).

4.1. La classe des mots affectifs mise à part, Beauzée procède à une classification des mots énonciatifs. Le premier critère qui permet de diviser les mots énonciatifs en deux séries (dont chacune comprend plusieurs classes) est celui de la déclinabilité des mots[35], à savoir

[35] «Un simple coup d'œil jeté sur les différentes espèces de mots, & sur l'unanimité des

la possession (ou non-possession) de caractéristiques morphologiques marquant les nombres, les cas, les genres, les personnes, les temps, les modes et la diathèse. Les quatre classes de mots déclinables (les *noms*, les *pronoms*, les *adjectifs* et les *verbes*) n'ont pas seulement en commun le trait formel de la déclinabilité: elles doivent aussi avoir

«une signification fondamentale commune, au moins jusqu'à un certain point: une propriété matérielle qui leur est commune, suppose nécessairement quelque chose de commun dans leur nature; & la nature des signes consiste dans leur signification. Mais il est certain qu'on ne peut nombrer que des êtres; & par conséquent il semble nécessaire de conclure que la signification fondamentale, commune aux quatre espèces de *Mots* déclinables, consiste à présenter à l'esprit les idées des êtres, soit réels soit abstraits, qui peuvent être les objets de notre pensée» (Mot, *E.M.*, tome II, p. 671).

4.2. Parmi les mots énonciatifs déclinables, une distinction est faite entre les noms et les pronoms d'une part, et entre les adjectifs et les verbes d'autre part. Cette distinction est basée sur un critère ontologique, à savoir la *détermination* ou l'*indétermination* des «êtres» désignés par ces classes de mots: les noms et les pronoms présentent à l'esprit des êtres déterminés, c'est-à-dire qu'on peut leur associer une idée (par exemple celle de «*courir*»), représentée par un individu, ou une «monade» (*coureur*), à savoir la personne en train de courir (qui peut affirmer «*je cours*»)[36]. Les verbes et les adjectifs présentent à l'esprit des êtres indéterminés (par exemple *courir, courant*), qui peuvent devenir déterminés par l'adjonction d'un mot désignant un être déterminé (nom ou pronom). Dans le cas de la combinaison *nom + adjectif*, on obtient une nouvelle idée:

«L'unité d'objet qui résulte toujours de l'union de l'Adjectif avec le Nom, démontre que l'idée particulière qui constitue la signification individuelle de

usages de toutes les langues à cet égard, conduit naturellement à les partager en deux classes générales, caractérisées par des différences purement matérielles. La première classe comprend toutes les espèces de mots déclinables, je veux dire les noms, les pronoms, les adjectifs, & les verbes, qui, dans la plupart des langues, reçoivent à leurs terminaisons des changements qui désignent des idées accessoires de relation, ajoutées à l'idée principale de leur signification. La seconde classe renferme les espèces de mots indéclinables, c'est-à-dire, les adverbes, les prépositions, les conjonctions, & les interjections, qui gardent dans le discours une forme immuable, parce qu'ils expriment constamment une seule & même idée principale» (Identité, *E.M.*, tome II, p. 278). Ce critère de déclinabilité remonte à Varron (*De lingua latina*, liber VIII); cf. Taylor (1974).

[36] Comme le fait remarquer Beauzée, les noms présentent un être déterminé à l'aide d'une idée précise, alors que l'idée est «vague & indéfinie» dans les pronoms (Mot, *E.M.*, tome II, p. 573). Les pronoms ne présentent distinctement que l'idée d'une personne, éventuellement combinée avec l'idée d'un rapport de possession, ou avec l'idée d'interrogation, etc.

chaque Adjectif, est vraiment une idée partielle de la nature totale de cet objet unique exprimé par le concours des deux parties d'oraison. Quand je dis, par exemple, *loi*, je présente à l'esprit un objet unique déterminé, j'en présente un autre également unique & déterminé, quand je dis *loi évangélique*, un autre, quand je dis, *nos lois*. L'idée de *loi* se trouve pourtant toujours dans ces trois expressions: mais c'est une idée totale dans le premier exemple, & dans les deux autres ce n'est plus qu'une idée partielle, qui concourt à former l'idée totale, avec l'autre idée partielle qui constitue la signification propre, ou de l'Adjectif *évangélique* dans le second exemple, ou de l'Adjectif *nos* dans le troisième. Ce qui convient proprement à *nos lois*, ne peut convenir ni à la *loi évangélique*, ni à la *loi* en général; de même ce qui convient proprement à la *loi évangélique*, ne peut convenir ni à *nos lois* ni à la *loi* en général: c'est que ce sont des idées totales toutes différentes: mais ce qui est vrai de la *loi* en général, est vrai en particulier de la *loi évangélique* & de *nos lois*, parce que les idées ajoutées à celle de *loi* ne détruisent pas celle de *loi*, qui est toujours la même en soi» (Mot, *E.M.*, tome II, p. 575).

De la combinaison d'un nom ou pronom avec un verbe, il résulte une pensée. Les grammairiens de l'*Encyclopédie* n'ont pas considéré ce cas à l'intérieur de la théorie du mot, mais ils l'ont étudié dans l'optique de l'analyse syntaxique des propositions en sujet et prédicat. Beauzée insiste sur le caractère secondaire du verbe et de l'adjectif par rapport au nom et au pronom: c'est *par imitation* que le verbe et l'adjectif s'accordent (respectivement en nombre, personne et genre — si on inclut les participes passés parmi les formes verbales —; en genre et en nombre) avec les noms et les pronoms avec lesquels ils concourent pour exprimer une pensée ou idée totale[37]. Les noms et les pronoms ont donc comme *corrélatifs* (ce terme est employé dans l'article «Mot») les verbes et les adjectifs.

Alors que les noms, les pronoms, les adjectifs et les verbes expriment des êtres dénombrables, déterminés dans le cas des noms et des pronoms, indéterminés dans le cas des adjectifs et des verbes, la caractéristique du *genre* permet de séparer les noms et les pronoms. Dans le cas des noms, le genre est fixé par l'usage ou déterminé par l'idée de leur nature[38]:

[37] On voit ici comment cette analyse, basée sur l'unité de l'objet signifié, permet de segmenter l'énoncé en constituants (en l'occurrence, des groupes nominaux).

[38] D'après la nature des êtres désignés par les noms, ceux-ci sont divisés en noms substantifs et noms abstractifs. D'après la nature individualisante ou généralisante du renvoi, les noms sont divisés en noms propres et noms appellatifs. Ces derniers sont subdivisés en génériques et spécifiques: «dans les Noms génériques, l'idée déterminante est celle d'une nature commune à toutes les espèces comprises sous un même genre, & à tous les individus de chacune de ces espèces; dans les Noms spécifiques, l'idée déterminante est celle d'une nature qui n'est commune qu'aux individus d'une seule espèce» (Mot, *E.M.*, tome II, p. 573).

«Chaque Nom a un Genre fixe & déterminé par l'usage, ou par la nature de l'objet nommé, ou par le choix libre de celui qui parle: ainsi, *pater*, père, est du masculin, *mater*, mère, est du féminin, par nature; *baculus*, bâton, est du masculin, *mensa*, table, est du féminin, par usage; *finis* en latin, *duché* en françois, sont du masculin ou du féminin, au gré de celui qui parle» (Mot, *E.M.*, tome II, p. 573).

Le pronom, par contre, a un genre déterminé par son emploi discursif:

«Les Pronoms au contraire n'ont point de Genre fixe; de sorte que, sous la même terminaison ou sous des terminaisons différentes, ils sont tantôt d'un Genre & tantôt d'un autre, non au gré de celui qui parle, mais selon le Genre même du Nom auquel le Pronom a rapport: ainsi, ἐγώ en grec, *ego* en latin, *ich* en allemand, *io* en italien, *je* en françois, sont masculins dans la bouche d'un homme, & féminins dans celle d'une femme: au contraire, *il* est toujours masculin, & *elle* toujours féminin, quoique ces deux *Mots*, au Genre près, ayent le même sens, ou plus tôt ne soient que le même Mot avec différentes inflexions & terminaisons» (Mot, *E.M.*, tome II, p. 573).

Un tel point de vue ne va pas sans difficultés: avec *je, ego,* ἐγώ, le genre du pronom dépend du sexe de la personne qui parle, mais ce n'est pas une caractéristique formelle du pronom. D'autre part, le genre du nom est conçu comme une marque soit morphologique, comme en latin[39], soit syntaxique, comme en français. Il est donc préférable de parler d'une *neutralisation formelle* caractérisant les pronoms vis-à-vis des noms, en ce qui concerne le marquage du genre[40]: alors que la

[39] Cette marque est parfois non transparente: *nauta*, mot de la première déclinaison latine en *-a*, est masculin; beaucoup de mots latins en *-us* (génitif *-i*) sont féminins (noms d'arbres, de villes, de pays, d'îles); la troisième et la cinquième déclinaison latine contiennent un très grand nombre de mots de genre différent.

[40] Du moins dans le cas des langues indo-européennes. Les langues sémitiques, par exemple, ont une forme distincte (masculine vs féminine) pour les pronoms de la seconde personne (et aussi pour ceux de la troisième, comme c'est le cas dans les langues indo-européennes); cf. Moscati (éd. 1964/1969²: 102-105) et Diakonoff (1965: 69-74). Voir aussi Hagège (1982: 96-97): «Il existe cependant des langues où les noms de discours ne suffisent pas: «je» et/ou «tu» distinguent formellement un masculin et un féminin en sémitique, khasi (Inde), thaï, koasati (Louisiane), biloxi (langue sioux éteinte où même l'âge était marqué aux deux premières personnes), certaines langues d'Australie». L'auteur montre aussi que la notion de personne est ambiguë et que son lien avec le pronom n'est pas transparent: «D'autre part, bien qu'il existe universellement des personnels ou expressions équivalentes, les coutumes restreignent souvent l'usage direct des 1re et 2e personnes: en Asie orientale, beaucoup de langues les ont tirées de noms supposant une hiérarchie (ex. «prince», «seigneur», «oncle» → «tu»; «serviteur» → «je»), et leur préfèrent généralement, dans le dialogue, d'autres procédés, comme en japonais l'intonation, les formes verbales de politesse (impliquant «tu») ou le choix même du verbe de modestie (impliquant «je»), tous procédés qui rendent *ego* omniprésent alors même qu'il n'y dit pas couramment «je». Au surplus, «je» et «tu» peuvent eux-mêmes, en français par exemple, renvoyer à des absents (ex. dialogue épistolaire), ou, à l'inverse, ne pas désigner des interlocuteurs (ex. *je* didactique dans *si je dis «non», je nie* ou *je* littéraire, non adressé à un *tu* précis, etc.), ou

distinction se conserve à la troisième personne, elle n'est plus marquée aux première et seconde personnes. On pourrait objecter que Beauzée a raison de postuler une distinction en genre pour les pronoms de la première et de la seconde personne: si les mots expriment une idée, l'idée exprimée par un pronom *renvoyant à* une personne mâle n'est pas la même que l'idée exprimée par un pronom renvoyant à une personne du sexe féminin. Mais à ce propos nous tenons à faire remarquer que la définition du pronom dit seulement que

«Les Pronoms sont des *Mots* qui présentent à l'esprit des êtres déterminés par l'idée précise de leur relation à l'acte de la parole» (Mot, *E.M.*, tome II, p. 574).

Il n'y est rien dit du sexe de la personne qui a une relation particulière à l'acte de la parole. Ainsi, une lecture systématique du texte de Beauzée nous apprend que dans l'idée exprimée par le pronom, le sexe de la personne n'est pas essentiellement présent; cet élément n'est d'ailleurs pas universellement marqué dans les langues naturelles. De cette façon, il n'aurait pas été nécessaire d'attribuer un genre flexible aux pronoms de la première et de la deuxième personne: c'est un élément redondant qu'il n'aurait pas fallu retenir du point de vue de la *systématique* et de l'*économie définitionnelles* de la théorie, d'autant plus que cet élément ne reçoit aucun appui formel.

4.3. Par cet enracinement dans l'acte de la parole, le pronom se rapproche du verbe: ces deux classes de mots ont un fondement discursif, formellement indiqué par la personne:

«On a pareillement, sous le nom de Personnes, rapporté les Pronoms à des classes différenciées par les diverses relations des êtres à l'acte de la parole (...) Les Personnes, par exemple, qui ne sont dans les Verbes que des terminaisons, suivent la relation du sujet à l'acte de la parole & les Verbes prennent telle ou telle terminaison personnelle selon cette relation de leurs sujets à l'acte de la parole: *ego Joannes vidi, tu Joannes vidisti, Joannes vidit*» (Mot, *E.M.*, tome II, p. 574).

Cette même donnée permet de séparer le verbe et l'adjectif, qui «présentent à l'esprit des êtres indéterminés» (Mot, *E.M.*, tome II, p. 574). En effet,

«L'Adjectif n'a reçu aucune variation relative aux Personnes qui caractérisent les Pronoms. Les Adjectifs mêmes dérivés des Verbes, qui, sous le nom de Parti-

être remplacés par autre chose: formules d'occultation comme *on*, *l'auteur de ces lignes*, etc., *nous* de majesté ou d'exposé savant, au sens de «je», ou *nous* familier (ex. *comment allons-nous?*), au sens de «tu». Enfin, il existe des emplois de «tu» ou «il» valant «je» (ex. russe parlé) et, dans certaines langues des «il» de politesse valant «tu» (p. 97).

cipes, réunissent en effet la double nature des deux parties d'oraison, n'ont reçu nulle part les inflexions personnelles» (Mot, *E.M.*, tome II, p. 574).

Si le verbe a des terminaisons personnelles, l'adjectif a des terminaisons marquant le genre, qui se rapportent à la nature du substantif auquel il est joint. Les adjectifs sont divisés en adjectifs *physiques* et en adjectifs *métaphysiques*:

«Les Adjectifs physiques sont ceux qui désignent les êtres indéterminés par une idée précise qui, étant ajoutée à celle de quelque nature déterminée, constitue avec elle une idée totale toute différente, dont la compréhension est augmentée. Tels sont les Adjectifs *pieux, rond, semblable*: car quand on dit un *homme pieux*, un *vase rond*, des *figures semblables*, on exprime des idées totales qui renferment, dans leur compréhension, plus d'attributs que celles que l'on exprime quand on dit simplement un *homme*, un *vase*, des *figures*. C'est que l'idée précise de la signification individuelle de cette sorte d'Adjectifs est une idée partielle de la nature totale. D'où il suit que, si l'on ne veut envisager les êtres dans le discours que comme revêtus de cet attribut exprimé nettement par l'Adjectif, il arrive souvent que l'Adjectif est employé comme un Nom, parce que l'attribut qui y est précis constitue alors toute la nature de l'objet que l'on a en vûe: c'est ainsi que nous disons le *bon*, le *vrai*, l'*honnête*, l'*utile*, les *françois*, les *romains*, les *africains*, &c. Les Adjectifs métaphysiques sont ceux qui désignent les êtres indéterminés par une idée précise qui, étant ajoutée à celle de quelque nature déterminée, constitue avec elle une idée totale dont la compréhension est toujours la même, mais dont l'étendue est restreinte. Tels sont les Adjectifs *le, ce, plusieurs*: car quand on dit *le roi, ce livre, plusieurs chevaux*, on exprime des idées totales qui renferment encore dans leur compréhension les mêmes attributs que celles que l'on exprime quand on dit simplement *roi, livre, cheval*, quoique l'étendue en soit plus restreinte; parce que l'idée précise de la signification individuelle de cette sorte d'Adjectifs, n'est que l'idée d'un point de vûe qui assigne seulement une quotité particulière d'individus. De là vient que, si l'on ne veut envisager dans le discours les êtres dont on parle que comme considérés sous ce point de vûe exprimé nettement par l'Adjectif, il arrive souvent que l'Adjectif est employé comme Pronom, parce que le point de vûe qui y est précis est alors la relation unique qui détermine l'être dont on parle; c'est ainsi que nous disons, *j'approuve CE que vous avez fait*» (Mot, *E.M.*, tome II, p. 575).

Comment faut-il comprendre cette distinction? Les adjectifs *physiques* augmentent la compréhension de l'idée exprimée par les substantifs avec lesquels ils sont associés; quant à l'extension de l'idée, celle-ci peut être restreinte (ce qui est le cas quand l'adjectif exprime une caractéristique qui n'est pas commune à tous les individus compris sous l'idée exprimée par le substantif; exemple: *homme blanc*), ou elle peut être conservée (quand l'adjectif exprime une caractéristique tautologique de l'idée exprimée par le substantif auquel l'adjectif est lié, comme dans *cercle rond*, ou quand l'adjectif exprime une caractéristique non analytique qui a, par contingence, la même extension que l'idée exprimée par le substantif auquel l'adjectif est associé, comme dans *homme mortel*). Les adjectifs métaphysiques, par contre, n'augmentent pas la compréhension, mais restreignent l'extension. Toutefois, la théorie de Beauzée manque de clarté à ce propos. Empêtré dans une vision logiciste des concepts («roi», «table», «maison», «livre», etc.), Beauzée confère à ceux-ci un statut linguistique d'occurrence réelle («quand on dit simplement *roi, livre, cheval*»), alors que leur réalisation discursive n'est jamais *roi, table, maison*, mais *un roi, le roi, la table/maison, une table/maison, des rois/tables/maisons, les rois/tables/maisons, plusieurs rois/tables/maisons, certains rois, certaines tables/maisons, la maison du roi, une maison de roi*, etc. Beauzée pose donc les mêmes formes (*roi, le roi*) au niveau des idées et au niveau de la parole. C'est ainsi que pour lui «*roi*» et «*le roi*» existent au niveau des idées *et* au niveau linguistique. Mais pour une langue qui connaît l'emploi d'articles, il faudrait distinguer entre l'intension et l'extension des *idées* (correspondant aux lexèmes figurant comme entrées dans le dictionnaire) et l'extension *en discours* (l'extensité)[41]. C'est par rapport à ce dernier niveau qu'il faut analyser les valeurs des articles (définis, indéfinis, partitifs, article zéro).

Revenons au verbe. Nous avons vu que le verbe emprunte ses caractéristiques formelles du nombre et du genre (dans le cas des participes) aux noms et pronoms auxquels il se rapporte[42]. En outre, le verbe a un lien direct avec l'acte de la parole, à l'aide duquel on peut comprendre la structure des personnes verbales. À l'intérieur de l'acte de parole, le verbe indique un être indéterminé sous son aspect d'*existence*. Cette existence est immédiatement liée au *temps* (il faut un temps, si minime soit-il, pour exister) et aux temps du verbe[43]:

[41] Pour la distinction entre compréhension, extension et extensité, voir Wilmet (1983).

[42] Point de vue qui suppose la priorité du sujet par rapport au verbe, mais qui rencontre des difficultés dans l'explication de formes comme *paenitet me*, *pluit*, italien *piove* ou *grandina*. La solution renaissanciste consistait à y voir des structures elliptiques: *Iovis pluit* (cf. Breva-Claramonte 1983: 57-60, 167-183).
Sur le problème de la directionnalité de l'accord du verbe avec le sujet, voir Matthews (1981: 102-117).

[43] Cf. Hagège (1982: 81) : «Leur affinité [= des marques d'aspect et du temps] avec le verbe, due sans doute au fait que ce qui se déroule dans un *espace temporel-notionnel* est précisément un procès (le plus souvent assumé par un prédicat verbal), se manifeste clairement: elles peuvent être amalgamées au verbe (ex. *il a/il eut*), affixées (ex. *il chante/il chantait*) (langues romanes, germaniques, sémitiques, bantoues, etc., avec variations segmentales et/ou prosodiques), relativement libres (ex. langues d'Afr. occ.), incidentes soit au verbe et au personnel à la fois, soit à ce dernier seul (variable parfois (ex. aymara (Pérou), takelma (Orégon)), selon l'aspect-temps et aussi les marques d'actance amalgamées), ou encore liées à la séquence».

«mais il est constant aussi qu'il n'y a pas une seule partie de la conjugaison du Verbe, qui n'exprime d'une manière ou d'une autre quelqu'un de ces rapports d'existence à une époque» (Mot, *E.M.*, tome II, p. 576).

En se référant à l'*Astronomie physique* d'Étienne Simon de Gamaches, Beauzée affirme que «le Temps est la succession même attachée à l'existence de la créature»[44]. Le temps est donc étroitement lié à l'essence du verbe, qui consiste à exprimer l'existence. Le temps du verbe est le seul indice dans une phrase qui permet de supposer une existence (soit réelle, soit idéelle): le verbe est ainsi la seule classe de mots qui déborde le contexte purement linguistique.

Le verbe est défini par Beauzée dans les termes suivants:

«les Verbes sont des *Mots* qui présentent à l'esprit des êtres indéterminés, désignés seulement par l'idée de l'existence sous un attribut» (Mot, *E.M.*, tome II, p. 576).

Contrairement aux Port-Royalistes, qui avaient défini le verbe par sa capacité d'établir une affirmation du locuteur, Beauzée, plus conceptualiste, définit le verbe par son contenu notionnel: tout verbe exprime *l'existence intellectuelle* d'un sujet. À l'idée d'existence intellectuelle peuvent s'ajouter des attributs, exprimés par des prédicats nominaux (*Jean est soldat*; *Jean est grand*), ou par le morphème lexical du verbe (*Jean réfléchit*).

4.4. Les mots indéclinables, correspondant à une idée objective immuable (Mot, *E.M.*, tome II, p. 577), comprennent trois classes de mots: les prépositions, les adverbes et les conjonctions. Cette tripartition repose sur des critères syntaxiques et sémantiques.

Prenons d'abord la distinction entre les adverbes et les prépositions d'une part, et les conjonctions d'autre part. À ce propos, Beauzée pose une distinction entre mots *supplétifs* (comprenant les adverbes et les prépositions et mots *discursifs* (comprenant les conjonctions): les mots supplétifs «suppléent» à la signification des mots auxquels ils se rapportent; les mots discursifs assurent la liaison entre des propositions. Cette distinction n'est ni très homogène (il aurait fallu opposer les mots indéclinables qui ne relient pas les propositions aux mots indéclinables qui le font), ni très exacte, étant donné que les conjonctions servent aussi à lier des composantes d'un *constituant* (exemple: *Jean et sa femme nous ont rendu visite hier soir*). Beauzée répliquerait qu'il s'agit d'un cas d'ellipse:

[44] Cf. «Mot» (*E.M.*, tome II, p. 576) et «Temps» (*E.M.*, tome III, p. 494-495). Pour une analyse de la théorie des temps verbaux chez Beauzée, voir Swiggers (1983a).

«Plusieurs Conjonctions semblent, au premier aspect, ne servir qu'à lier un *Mot* avec un autre: mais si l'on y prend garde de près, on verra qu'en effet elles servent à lier les propositions partielles qui constituent un même discours (...) Il ne peut donc y avoir de doute que dans le cas où divers attributs sont énoncés du même sujet, ou le même attribut de différents sujets; par exemple, *Cicéron étoit orateur ET philosophe*, *Lupus ET Agnus venerant*. Mais il est aisé de ramener à la loi commune les Conjonctions de ces exemples: le premier se réduit aux deux propositions liées, *Cicéron étoit orateur ET Cicéron étoit philosophe*, lesquelles ont un même sujet; le second veut dire pareillement, *Lupus venerat ET Agnus venerat*, les deux *Mots* attributifs *venerat* étant compris dans le pluriel *venerant*» (Mot, *E.M.*, tome II, p. 578)[45].

Par l'emploi de la notion d'ellipse, Beauzée fait de la conjonction un élément qui sert à lier des propositions, même si à un niveau «superficiel» la conjonction relie des composantes d'un constituant de phrase.

Les deux classes de mots supplétifs, l'adverbe et la préposition, sont apparentées formellement (certains adverbes sont composés à l'aide de prépositions) et sémantiquement (il y a une équivalence de sens entre l'adverbe et la construction *préposition + nom* de la même «racine» que l'adverbe).

«Par rapport aux Adverbes, c'est une observation importante, que l'on trouve dans une langue plusieurs Adverbes qui n'ont dans une autre langue aucun équivalent sous la même forme, mais qui s'y rendent par une préposition, avec un complément qui énonce la même idée qui constitue la signification individuelle de l'Adverbe; *eminus*, de loin, *cominus*, de près, *utrinque*, des deux côtés, &c.: on peut même regarder souvent comme synonymes dans une même langue les deux expressions, par l'Adverbe & par la Préposition avec son complément; *prudenter*, prudemment, ou *cum prudentiâ*, avec prudence»; «Mais il est constant qu'une préposition avec son complément est l'équivalent d'un adverbe, & que tout *Mot* qui est l'équivalent d'une Préposition avec son complément est un adverbe; d'où il suit que, quand on écriroit de suite *parconséquent*, il n'en seroit pas moins adverbe, parce que l'étymologie y trouveroit toujours les mêmes éléments, & la Logique le même sens» (Mot, *E.M.*, tome II, p. 577 et p. 579).

Mais dans la perspective de la construction de la phrase, l'adverbe et la préposition ont des fonctions très différentes. La préposition est un terme doublement corrélatif: elle établit un rapport direct avec le mot qui suit ou les mots qui suivent (*à demain, à la maison, vers la ville*, etc.) avec lequel (lesquels) elle constitue un syntagme. Elle établit aussi un rapport avec les mots qui la précèdent; ce rapport peut être un rapport

[45] Cette analyse par l'ellipse se heurte à quelques obstacles. Des phrases comme *Jean et Paul sont des frères; Jean et Paul se ressemblent* ne se laissent pas décomposer en deux unités conjointes. Ce problème a été relevé par Lakoff-Peters (1966) et par McCawley (1968: 148-155) dans leur critique de la grammaire transformationnelle.

direct (par exemple: *la maison de son directeur; les principes de la grammaire générative*) ou il peut être moins direct (*il la battait avec violence, assez régulièrement; il parla avec froideur; il s'en est allé, vers huit heures*). En termes plus formels, le rapport de la préposition avec ce qui la suit (en termes logiques, son «successeur») est un rapport intra-constituantiel, alors que le rapport avec son «antécédent» est soit un rapport intra-constituantiel, soit un rapport interconstituantiel (ceci est le cas quand l'antécédent est lui-même (une partie d') un autre constituant de phrase). L'explication de Beauzée, moins descriptive et plus philosophique, met en relief ce double rapport établi par la préposition, sans pourtant faire la distinction entre un rapport intra-constituantiel et un rapport interconstituantiel avec l'antécédent:

«Les Prépositions dans toutes les langues, exigent à leur suite un complément, sans lequel elles ne présentent à l'esprit qu'un sens vague & incomplet (...) L'application que l'on peut faire des mêmes Prépositions à une infinité de circonstances différentes, démontre que les rapports qu'elles désignent font abstraction de toute application, & que les termes en sont indéterminés (...) Nous pouvons donc conclure de ces observations, que *les Prépositions sont des* Mots *qui désignent des rapports généraux avec abstraction de tout terme antécédent & conséquent*. De là la nécessité de donner à la Préposition un complément qui en fixe le sens, qui par lui-même est vague & indéfini; c'est le terme conséquent du rapport envisagé vaguement dans la Préposition. De là encore le besoin de joindre la Préposition avec son complément, à un adjectif, ou à un verbe, ou à un nom appellatif, dont le sens général se trouve modifié & restreint par l'idée accessoire de ce rapport; l'adjectif, le verbe, ou le nom appellatif, en est le terme antécédent; *l'utilité DE la Métaphysique, courageux SANS témérité, aimer AVEC fureur*; chacune de ces phrases exprime un rapport complet: on y voit l'antécédent, *l'utilité, courageux, aimer*; le conséquent, *la Métaphysique, témérité, fureur*; & l'exposant, *de, sans, avec*» (Mot, *E.M.*, tome II, p. 577).

Les exemples de Beauzée contiennent donc des prépositions entretenant un rapport intra-constituantiel avec le terme antécédent (*l'utilité de la métaphysique*) et des prépositions entretenant un rapport interconstituantiel avec le terme antécédent (*aimer avec fureur*).

L'adverbe a deux traits en commun avec la préposition: comme elle, il exprime un rapport général et présuppose un terme antécédent[46]. Mais

[46] «Ne nous contentons pas d'observer la différence des Prépositions & des Adverbes; voyons encore ce qu'il y a de commun entre ces deux espèces: l'une & l'autre énonce encore un rapport général, c'est l'idée générique fondamentale des deux»; «Ceci nous conduit donc à un principe essenciel: c'est que tout Adverbe, ainsi que toute phrase qui renferme une Préposition avec son complément, sont des expressions qui se rapportent essencielle-

la différence réside dans le fait que l'adverbe n'a pas besoin d'un terme conséquent:

«Les Adverbes renferment dans leur signification le terme conséquent du rapport. Les Adverbes sont donc des *Mots* qui expriment des rapports généraux, déterminés par la désignation du terme conséquent» (Mot, *E.M.*, tome II, p. 577).

Mais terme conséquent par rapport à quoi? Par rapport au verbe? Beauzée écarte cette interprétation en se fondant sur une étymologie erronée du mot *adverbe*[47]. Par rapport à la phrase entière? Mais ne faut-il pas distinguer ici entre les adverbes qui se rapportent au sens de la phrase entière (exemple: *il a été puni sévèrement de ses crimes*) et ceux qui se rapportent à la phrase comme ensemble locutionnaire ou illocutionnaire (*Bien sûr, Jean est revenu hier; Malheureusement, les choses ne sont pas toujours aussi simples; Ainsi, je vous nomme secrétaire d'Etat*)[48]? Beauzée se borne à noter que

«L'Adverbe supplée aussi souvent à la signification des adjectifs, & même à celle d'autres adverbes, qu'à celle des verbes» (Mot, *E.M.*, tome II, p. 578).

ment à un *Mot* antécédent dans l'ordre analytique, & qu'elles ajoûtent à la signification de ce *Mot* une idée de relation qui en fait envisager le sens tout autrement qu'il ne se présente dans le *Mot* seul: *aimer tendrement* ou *avec tendresse*, c'est autre chose qu'*aimer* tout simplement. Si l'on envisage donc la Préposition & l'Adverbe sous ce point de vûe commun, on peut dire que ce sont des *Mots* supplétifs, puisqu'ils servent également à suppléer les idées accessoires qui ne se trouvent point comprises dans la signification des *Mots* auxquels on les rapporte, & qu'ils ne peuvent servir qu'à cette fin» (Mot, *E.M.*, tome II, p. 578).

47 «À l'occasion de cette application nécessaire de l'Adverbe à un *Mot* antécédent, j'observerai que l'étymologie du nom *Adverbe*, telle que la donne Sanctius (*Minerva III*.13), n'est bonne qu'autant que le nom latin *verbum* sera pris dans son sens propre pour signifier *Mot*, & non pas *Verbe*» (Mot, *E.M.*, tome II, p. 578).

48 Sur les différents types d'adverbes et de compléments prépositionnels à valeur adverbiale, voir nos remarques dans Swiggers (1982b: 33-34). Pour des études récentes sur les fonctions des adverbes en anglais et en français, voir Buysschaert (1983) et Melis (1983). La source d'inspiration des études sur les différents types d'adverbes est Jackendoff (1972: 47-107). Voir également les remarques de Hagège (1982: 89-90): «On appelle «adverbes» ... un ensemble de lexèmes fonctionnellement hétérogènes: compléments circonstanciels (ex. *où ?, hier, mal*), déterminants d'adjectifs ou d'autres adverbes (ex. *très beau, assez tôt*), régissants de noms (ex. *même Jean dort*), régis de relateurs (ex. *dès demain*), opérateurs énonciatifs (ex. *peut-être*), connecteurs entre énoncés (ex. *en effet*). Aucun critère ne peut les regrouper: la non-occurrence en contiguïté est contredite par des cas comme *plus loin*; la liberté de position est très variable en français, et soumise en chinois aux mêmes contraintes que pour les autres types de mots; le rôle de circonstants (qui fait même, dans la tradition anglaise, parler de «fonction adverbiale») ne concerne pas les éléments tels qu'*aussi* ou *presque*, traités comme adverbes alors qu'ils constituent, par leurs propriétés, une catégorie spéciale de *modificateurs*».

L'adverbe — en tant que terme conséquent — se caractérise donc par une corrélativité unilatérale: celle avec un autre mot dans la phrase, ou avec la phrase entière. Parfois l'adverbe a un terme conséquent (son *régime*): ceci est le cas lorsque l'idée du terme conséquent peut être rendue par un nom appellatif ou par un adjectif dont la signification, trop générale ou essentiellement relative, exige l'addition d'un nom qui la détermine ou la complète (exemples latins: *ubi terrarum, tunc temporis*).

4.5. Dans le schéma ci-joint, nous résumons la classification des mots *énonciatifs*, en distinguant les critères formels et les critères sémantiques qui ont permis à Beauzée d'opérer des divisions, le plus souvent binaires.

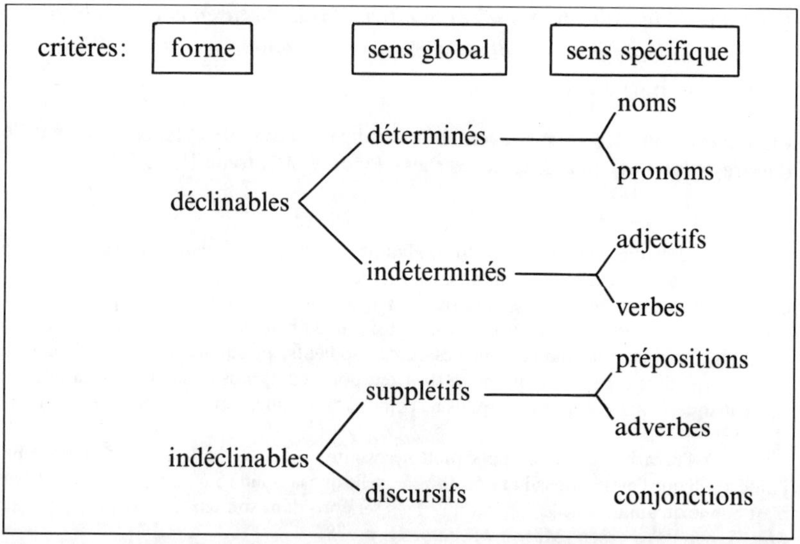

5. De Maupas aux Idéologues, le schéma des parties du discours occupe la partie centrale dans les grammaires. La syntaxe, devenant plus autonome — mais l'évolution n'est certes pas rectiligne —, se construit par rapport à la morphologie, en plusieurs étapes: extension du nom en groupe nominal, analyse du régime des verbes, le lien perçu entre les adverbes simples et les expressions modificatives («compléments circonstanciels»), etc. Cette attention croissante accordée aux relations entre classes de mots et structures syntagmatiques, résulte dans une approche plus formelle et moins sémantique des parties du discours: *il importe moins de dire ce qu'un nom signifie que de préciser comment il s'insère dans un discours.* En outre, les données du français sont examinées en elles-mêmes, et non en fonction d'une théorie générale sur le sémantisme des langues. Mais comme la langue est toujours envisagée par rapport à la pensée dont elle est le signe, la définition des parties du discours conserve une base notionnelle (appuyée par des considérations formelles). Une des conséquences de cette approche notionnelle (cf. Lyons 1968: 317-333) est l'obstination des grammairiens — à quelques rares exceptions près — à proclamer la fixité des classes de mots. Ce manque d'empirisme rendait impossible l'étude systématique des enchevêtrements de la syntaxe, de la morphologie, et parfois aussi des données phoniques, concourant à l'expression d'un sens. Mais peut-on reprocher aux grammairiens de l'âge classique — dont les réflexions sur les classes de mots sont souvent plus intéressantes que celles de bon nombre de grammairiens du XIXe et du XXe siècle — de n'avoir pu résoudre ce qui est encore aujourd'hui le problème essentiel de toute théorie grammaticale[49]?

Références

Aarsleff, H. 1975. «The eighteenth century, including Leibniz». T.A. Sebeok ed., *Current trends in linguistics*, vol. 13: *Historiography of linguistics*, 383-479. The Hague: Mouton.

Aarsleff, H. 1979. «Supplementary bibliography of recent studies in the historiography of linguistics relating to the eighteenth century, including Leibniz». *Histoire, Épistémologie, Langage* 1:2. 41-73.

Aerts, J. 1981. *Étude sur l'œuvre grammaticale du Père Buffier*. Leuven (mémoire de licence, K.U.L.).

Auroux, S. 1979. *La sémiotique des encyclopédistes. Essai d'épistémologie historique des sciences du langage*. Paris: Payot.

Benveniste, E. 1946. «Structure des relations de personne dans le verbe». *Bulletin de la Société de Linguistique de Paris* 43. 1-12 (repris dans *Problèmes de linguistique générale I*, 225-236. Paris: Gallimard, 1966).

Brauße, U. 1983. «Die Bedeutung des Verbs. Semantische Theorien des 17. und 18. Jahrhunderts in Port-Royal und bei Du Marsais». *Beiträge zur Romanischen Philologie* 22. 247-266.

Brekle, H.E. 1969. c.r. de Chomsky (1966). *Linguistics* 49. 74-91.

Breva-Claramonte, M. 1983. *Sanctius' theory of language. A contribution to the history of Renaissance linguistics*. Amsterdam: J. Benjamins.

Brunot, F. 1909-1915. *Histoire de la langue française des origines à nos jours*. Tome III: *La formation de la langue classique (1600-1660)*. Première partie (1909). Deuxième partie (1911). Tome IV: *La langue classique (1660-1715)*. Première partie (1913). Deuxième partie (1915). Paris: A. Colin (réédition Paris: A. Colin, 1966).

[49] Voir à ce propos les remarques pénétrantes de Hagège (1984).

Buffier, Cl. 1709. *Grammaire françoise sur un plan nouveau, pour en rendre les principes plus clairs et la pratique plus aisée, contenant divers traités sur la grammaire en général, sur l'usage, sur la beauté des langues et sur la manière de les apprendre, sur le style, sur l'orthographe*. Paris: N. Le Clerc.

Buysschaert, J. 1982. *Criteria for the classification of English adverbials*. Brussel: Paleis der Academiën.

Chevalier, J.-Cl. 1968. *Histoire de la syntaxe. Naissance de la notion de complément dans la grammaire française (1530-1750)*. Genève: Droz.

Chiflet, L. 1659. *Essay d'une parfaite grammaire de la langue françoise Ou le Lecteur trouvera, en bel ordre, tout ce qui est de plus necessaire, de plus curieux, & de plus elegant, en la Pureté, en l'Orthographe, & en la Prononciation de cette Langue*. Anvers: Jacques Van Meurs.

Chomsky, N. 1966. *Cartesian linguistics. A chapter in the history of rationalist thought*. New York-London: Harper & Row (traduction française *La linguistique cartésienne, suivi de La nature formelle du langage*, Paris: Seuil, 1969).

Diakonoff, I.M. 1965. *Semito-Hamitic languages. An essay in classification*. Moscou: Nauka.

Dominicy, M. 1977. «Les parties du discours dans la grammaire de Port-Royal». S. De Vriendt - Ch. Peeters éds, *Linguistics in Belgium* 1, 25-37. Bruxelles: Didier.

Dominicy, M. 1979. «Additions à la bibliographie de Charles Porset sur les sciences du langage de Port-Royal aux Idéologues (1660-1818)». *Dix-huitième siècle* 11. 431-436.

Dominicy, M. 1984. *La naissance de la grammaire moderne. Langage, logique et philosophie à Port-Royal*. Bruxelles: Mardaga.

Donzé, R. 1967. *La Grammaire générale et raisonnée de Port-Royal. Contribution à l'histoire des idées grammaticales en France*. Bern: Francke (deuxième édition: 1971).

Droixhe, D. 1978. *La linguistique et l'appel de l'histoire (1600-1800). Rationalisme et révolutions positivistes*. Genève: Droz.

Duclos, Ch.P. 1754. *Remarques sur la Grammaire générale et raisonnée de Port-Royal*. Paris: Prault fils.

Durand, J. 1977. «Some aspects of reference and predication in the *Grammaire générale et raisonnée* and in the Port-Royal *Logique*». *Studies in Language* 1. 321-336.

Encyclopédie méthodique: Grammaire et littérature. Éditée par Beauzée et Marmontel. 1782-1786. Paris-Liège: Panckoucke et Plomteux (3 volumes).

Féraud, J.-F. 1761. *Dictionnaire grammatical de la langue françoise*. Avignon: Girard (cinquième édition Paris: Delalain, 1788).

Foucault, M. 1966. *Les mots et les choses. Une archéologie des sciences humaines*. Paris: Gallimard.

Hagège, Cl. 1982. *La structure des langues*. Paris: Presses universitaires de France.

Hagège, Cl. 1984. «Sur les trois structurations de l'énoncé dans les langues humaines». *Lingua e Stile* 19. 349-379.

Hall, R.A. 1969. «Some recent studies on Port-Royal and Vaugelas». *Acta Linguistica Hafniensia* 12. 290-303.

Hanse, J. 1962. «La contribution belge à la définition du 'bon usage'». *Cahiers de l'Association internationale des Études françaises* 14. 25-37.

Harnois, G. 1928. *Les théories du langage en France de 1660 à 1821*. Paris: Les Belles Lettres.

Jackendoff, R. 1972. *Semantic interpretation in generative grammar*. Cambridge, Mass.: MIT Press.

Joly, A. 1980. «Le problème de l'article et sa solution dans les grammaires de l'époque classique». *Langue française* 48. 16-27.

Kretzmann, N. 1975. «Transformationalism and the Port-Royal Grammar». J. Rieux - B.E. Rollin, *General and Rational grammar: The Port-Royal Grammar by Antoine Arnauld and Claude Lancelot*, 176-197. The Hague-Paris: Mouton.

Lakoff, G. - S. Peters. 1966. *Phrasal conjunction and symmetric predicates*. Harvard University: Computation Laboratory (Mathematical Linguistics and Automatic Translation, Report n° NSF-17).

Loiseau, A. 1875. *Histoire des progrès de la grammaire en France, depuis l'époque de la Renaissance jusqu'à nos jours*. Paris: Thorin.

Lyons, J. 1968. *Introduction to theoretical linguistics*. Cambridge: University Press.

Mariën, S. 1982. *Étude sur l'œuvre grammaticale de Pierre Restaut*. Leuven (mémoire de licence, K.U.L.).

Marzys, Z. 1984. *La Préface aux Remarques sur la langue françoyse de Claude Favre de Vaugelas*. Neuchâtel-Genève: Faculté des Lettres de l'Université & Droz.

Matthews, P.H. 1981. *Syntax*. Cambridge: University Press.

McCawley, J.D. 1968. «The role of semantics in a grammar». E. Bach - R. Harms eds., *Universals in linguistic theory*, 124-169. New York: Holt, Rinehart & Winston.

Melis, L. 1983. *Les circonstants et la phrase. Étude sur la classification et la systématique des compléments circonstanciels en français moderne*. (Symbolae Facultatis Litterarum et Philosophiae Lovaniensis, series A, 13). Louvain: Presses Universitaires.

Mertens, J. 1968. *Contribution à l'étude de la terminologie grammaticale française. La nomenclature du verbe chez les grammairiens français du XVIIe siècle*. Leuven (thèse de doctorat).

Michael, I. 1970. *English grammatical categories and the tradition to 1800*. Cambridge: University Press.

Missinne, E. 1984. *Étude de la grammaire française (1632-1640) d'Antoine Oudin*. Leuven (mémoire de licence, K.U.L.).

Moscati, S. ed. 1964. *An introduction to the comparative grammar of the Semitic languages. Phonology and morphology*. Wiesbaden: O. Harrassowitz (1969^2).

Murat, M. 1979. «La théorie du nom adjectif et substantif dans la *Grammaire* et la *Logique* de Port-Royal». *Le français moderne* 47. 335-352.

Nuchelmans, G. 1980. *Late-scholastic and humanist theories of the proposition*. Amsterdam: North-Holland Publishing Company.

Ong, W.J. 1958. *Ramus, method and the decay of dialogue. From the art of discourse to the art of reason*. Cambridge, Mass. - London: Harvard University Press (1983²).

Oudin, A. 1632. *Grammaire françoise, rapportée au langage du temps*. Paris: Pierre Billaine.

Padley, A.G. 1976. *Grammatical theory in Western Europe 1500-1700. The Latin tradition*. Cambridge: University Press.

Pariente, J.-Cl. 1982. «Sur la théorie du verbe chez Condillac». J. Sgard éd., *Condillac et les problèmes du langage*, 257-274. Genève: Slatkine.

Porset, Ch. 1977. «Grammatista philosophans. Les sciences du langage de Port-Royal aux Idéologues (1660-1818). Bibliographie». A. Joly - J. Stéfanini éds, *La grammaire générale des Modistes aux Idéologues*, 11-95. Lille: Presses universitaires.

Port-Royal (Arnauld et Lancelot). 1660. *Grammaire generale et raisonnée Contenant Les fondemens de l'art de parler expliquez d'une maniere claire & naturelle; Les raisons de ce qui est commun à toutes les langues, & des principales differences qui s'y rencontrent; Et plusieurs remarques nouvelles sur la Langue Françoise*. Paris: Pierre le Petit (édition critique: *Grammaire générale ou raisonnée, ou, la Grammaire de Port-Royal*, éd. par H.E. Brekle, Stuttgart-Bad Cannstatt: F. Frommann Verlag - G. Holzboog, 1966).

Port-Royal (Arnauld et Nicole). 1662. *La logique ou l'Art de Penser, contenant outre les Regles communes, plusieurs observations nouvelles propres à former le iugement*. Paris: Guignart-Savreux-de Launay (édition critique par B. Baron von Freytag Löringhoff - H.E. Brekle, Stuttgart-Bad Cannstatt: F. Frommann Verlag - G. Holzboog, 1965-1967).

Régaldo, M. 1970. «Matériaux pour une bibliographie de l'idéologie et des idéologues». *Répertoire analytique de la littérature française* 1:1. 35-50; 1:2. 27-41.

Régnier-Desmarais, F.-S. 1705. *Traité de la grammaire françoise*. Paris: J.-B. Coignard (1706²).

Restaut, P. 1730. *Principes généraux et raisonnés de la grammaire françoise avec des observations sur l'orthographe, les accents, la ponctuation et la prononciation*. Paris: J. Desaint.

Robinet, A. 1978. *Le langage à l'âge classique*. Paris: Klincksieck.

Scheemaeker, N. 1983. *Étude comparative des ouvrages grammaticaux d'Irson, de Filz et de Foigny*. Leuven (mémoire de licence, K.U.L.).

Slatkine, M.-E. 1971. *Grammairiens et théoriciens français de la Renaissance à la fin de l'époque classique, 1521-1715*. Genève: Slatkine.

Stéfanini, J. 1984. «Méthode et pédagogie dans les grammaires françaises de la première moitié du XVIIe siècle». P. Swiggers éd. 1984. 35-48.

Stengel, E. 1890. *Chronologisches Verzeichnis französischer Grammatiken vom Ende des 14. bis zum Ausgange des 18. Jahrhunderts nebst Angabe der bisher ermittelten Fundorte derselben*. Oppeln: E. Franck's Buchhandlung.

Stengel, E. - H.J. Niederehe. 1976. *Chronologisches Verzeichnis* ... (cf. Stengel 1890). Neu herausgegeben mit einem Anhang. Amsterdam: J. Benjamins.

Swiggers, P. 1979. c.r. de Stengel-Niederehe 1976. *Lingvisticae Investigationes* 3. 192-204.

Swiggers, P. 1980. «Durand on Port-Royal». *Studies in Language* 4. 125-130.

Swiggers, P. 1981a. «La théorie du nom et de l'adjectif dans la *Grammaire* et la *Logique* de Port-Royal». *Le français moderne* 49. 234-242.

Swiggers, P. 1981b. «La théorie du verbe dans la *Grammaire* de Port-Royal». *Zeitschrift für französische Sprache und Literatur* 91. 357-362.

Swiggers, P. 1982a. «Le pronom relatif chez Chiflet». *Le français moderne* 50. 140-143.

Swiggers, P. 1982b. c.r. de Matthews 1981. *Kratylos* 27. 29-36.

Swiggers, P. 1983a. «Beauzée et le système des temps en français». *Acta Linguistica Hafniensia* 18. 95-111.

Swiggers, P. 1983b. «Grammaire et théorie du langage chez Buffier». *Dix-huitième siècle* 15. 285-293.

Swiggers, P. 1983c. «Studies on the French eighteenth-century grammatical tradition». *Studies on Voltaire and the Eighteenth Century* 219. 273-280.

Swiggers, P. 1983d. «La théorie syntaxique dans l'*Encyclopédie*». *Lingua e Stile* 18. 161-176.

Swiggers, P. 1984a. *Les conceptions linguistiques des encyclopédistes. Étude sur la constitution d'une théorie de la grammaire au siècle des Lumières*. Heidelberg-Leuven: J. Groos & Leuven University Press.

Swiggers, P. 1984b. «Méthode et description grammaticale chez Denis Vairasse d'Allais». P. Swiggers éd. 1984. 68-87.

Swiggers, P. 1984c. «Vairasse d'Allais et sa grammaire française à l'usage des Anglais». *Le français moderne* 52. 221-224.

Swiggers, P. éd. 1984. *Grammaire et méthode au XVIIe siècle*. Leuven: Peeters.

Swiggers, P. 1985a. «L'article en français: Histoire d'un problème grammatical». *Revue de Linguistique romane* 49. 379-409.

Swiggers, P. 1985b. «Une étape importante dans l'histoire de la grammaire française: les *Principes* de Restaut». *Studia Neophilologica* 57. 219-226.

Swiggers, P. - F.J. Mertens. 1983. «La *Grammaire générale et raisonnée* de Port-Royal: Notes bibliographiques». *Historiographia Linguistica* 10. 357-362.

Swiggers, P. - F.J. Mertens. 1984. «La grammaire française au XVIIe siècle. Bibliographie raisonnée». P. Swiggers éd. 1984. 95-110.

Taylor, D. 1974. *Declinatio: A study of the linguistic theory of Marcus Terentius Varro*. Amsterdam: J. Benjamins,.

Uitti, K.D. 1969. «Descartes and Port-Royal in two diverse retrospects». *Romance Philology* 23. 79-85.

Vairasse d'Allais, D. 1681. *Grammaire methodique contenant en abregé les principes de cet art Et les Regles les plus necessaires de la Langue Françoise dans un ordre clair & naturel, Avec de nouvelles observations & des caracteres nouveaux pour en faciliter la prononciation, sans rien changer d'essentiel dans l'orthographe ni dans l'etymologie des mots*. Paris: Chez l'Auteur le Sr D.V. d'Allais.

Vandekerckhove, J. 1984. *Étude sur le Traité de la grammaire françoise de F.S. Régnier-Desmarais*. Leuven (mémoire de licence, K.U.L.).

Vorlat, E. 1975. *The development of English grammatical theory 1586-1737*. Leuven: University Press.

Webster, J. 1984. *William Temple's Analysis of Sir Philip Sidney's Apology for poetry. An edition and translation*. Binghamton: Center for Medieval & Early Renaissance Studies.

Wilmet, M. 1983. «Les déterminants du nom en français. Essai de synthèse». *Langue française* 57. 15-33.

Winkler, E. 1912. *La doctrine grammaticale française d'après Maupas et Oudin.* Halle: M. Niemeyer.

Wüest, J. 1978. c.r. de Stengel-Niederehe 1976. *Vox Romanica* 37. 352-353.

Zimmer, K.E. 1968. c.r. de Chomsky (1966). *International Journal of American Linguistics* 34. 290-303.

André MARTINET
(École des Hautes Études à la Sorbonne)

QUE FAIRE DU «MOT»?

Le *Petit Larousse illustré*, dans son édition de 1972, dit du terme *mot* qu'il est «un son ou groupe de sons servant à désigner un être, une idée» et, plus loin, «une lettre ou un ensemble de lettres délimités par deux blancs, qui représentent ce son». Il y a, on le sait, possibilité de contradiction entre les deux éléments de la définition: un *chemin de fer* désigne un objet bien défini correspondant à une «idée» unique, dans ce sens qu'on ne saurait définir un quelconque des composants du signifiant sans détruire le concept: un **chemin creux ... de fer*, **un chemin de fer blanc*; pourtant il est composé de trois «mots» séparés par des blancs. Comme cette définition correspond bien à l'usage, il nous faut diagnostiquer ici un cas de polysémie, ce qu'indique d'ailleurs le dictionnaire en cause, en plaçant, entre les deux éléments de la définition, une double barre verticale.

La polysémie est une condition *sine qua non* de l'utilisation du langage humain: celui-ci, on le sait, doit permettre de communiquer une infinité d'expériences différentes au moyen d'un vocabulaire limité. Il faut donc adapter le vocabulaire aux besoins en confiant à chaque unité signifiante le soin de signifier du partiellement différent en faisant confiance au contexte pour orienter l'auditeur ou le lecteur. Il ne semble pas qu'on puisse refuser cette ressource de la langue à ceux qui exposent les résultats de leur recherche. On m'a reproché d'avoir, dans les *Éléments de linguistique générale*, utilisé le terme «fonction» avec des valeurs très différentes: d'une part, avec sa valeur ordinaire, dans *fonction communicative du langage*; d'autre part, dans *fonction grammaticale*, pour référer, par exemple, au sujet ou à l'objet. Je n'ai cependant pas jugé bon de modifier sur ce point ma terminologie, car j'estime que dans le cas en question, les contextes permettent toujours d'éviter l'ambiguïté. Dire, comme le font certains, «cas» pour «fonction grammaticale» est très déroutant pour qui attend d'un cas qu'il se manifeste nécessairement au moyen d'une désinence. Cela ne permet pas d'éliminer toute polysémie, à moins de retirer à «cas» sa valeur ordinaire d'occurrence, ce qui est évidemment impensable.

Si donc le problème que soulève «mot» tenait uniquement aux deux emplois, éventuellement contradictoires, signalés ci-dessus, on pourrait aisément le résoudre en recommandant, pour le second, l'adjonction d'«écrit» partout où le contexte ne lève pas l'ambiguïté.

Le vrai problème de «mot» n'est donc pas là. Il est dans l'impossibilité où nous sommes de définir exactement 1° ce qui est un ou plusieurs mots dans la chaîne du discours, c'est-à-dire en syntagmatique, 2° ce qui est un ou plusieurs mots dans le lexique, c'est-à-dire en paradigmatique[1].

On nous dit que le mot sert «à désigner un être, une idée». Comme toute définition présentée en termes sémantiques, celle-ci est inutilisable en pratique, à moins que nous en déduisions des implications qui pourront nous permettre de nous prononcer dans une situation donnée. Qu'il s'agisse de la désignation d'un référent particulier et unique dans la réalité perceptible («un être» de la définition du *Larousse*) ou de la conception qu'on se fait de quelque chose de particulier et d'unique, existant ou imaginé («une idée» de la même définition), l'accent est mis sur l'unicité du signifié. Cette unicité impliquera nécessairement qu'une détermination, dans un contexte langagier, ne pourra porter que sur cette désignation comme un tout, et en aucune façon sur quelque aspect particulier de l'entité en cause. Ceci vaut même si la désignation comporte des éléments auxquels on pourrait attribuer un sens particulier s'ils n'étaient là que pour cerner l'individualité du signifié: si je parle d'une *ferme pilote*, je ne me réfère pas à deux objets distincts, une ferme et un pilote, mais à un seul, une ferme, d'un type particulier, pour laquelle je ne trouve pas, dans la langue, de désignation simple, ce qui m'oblige à en fabriquer une par détermination d'un terme par un autre. Mais une fois ceci accompli, il ne peut plus être question de dissocier les deux termes sans détruire la nouvelle désignation. La marque la plus décisive d'une telle dissociation serait la détermination individuelle de chacun des deux éléments, par exemple, dans *une ferme de brique plus pilote* où l'on rétablirait l'identité distincte de la ferme et de la notion de pilote. Le test de l'absence de déterminations particulières établit le

[1] Pour une orientation bibliographique sur le mot, voir la bibliographie sélective à la fin de ce volume.
Pour l'optique très particulière adoptée ci-dessus selon laquelle on n'a intérêt à ne retenir le terme qu'en référence à des situations bien définies, l'auteur renvoie à ses travaux où se trouve notamment discutée et écartée l'idée qu'on pourrait tenter d'établir un parallélisme entre le phonème comme somme de traits distinctifs et le «mot» comme somme de traits de sens, y compris ceux qu'apportent les modalités et le connecteur éventuel; voir surtout Martinet (1965) et Martinet (1985: §§3.44 à 3.61). Sur *monème* et *synthème*, voir Martinet (1985: §§ 3.1 à 3.10).

caractère de «mot» de l'ensemble *ferme pilote*. Même sans le trait d'union qui en ferait un «mot écrit», on pourra le caractériser comme un «mot composé» au même titre qu'*autoroute* ou *timbre-poste*.

Ce test de non-détermination vaut, bien entendu, aussi bien pour les dérivés que pour les composés. On voit mal en effet comment on pourrait déterminer un affixe qui, de fondation pour ainsi dire, ne vaut que par sa contribution à la valeur d'un ensemble. Sans doute, ne prétend-on pas ici que ce test permette toujours de se prononcer à coup sûr sur ce qui est «mot composé» et ce qui est combinaison de «mots». Nous sommes sûrs de nous en ce qui concerne *pomme de terre* ou *chemin de fer*. Pour un complexe *général de brigade*, où le test s'applique également, certains pourraient faire valoir que le sens de l'ensemble se déduisant totalement de la somme de ceux des trois éléments, ce qui n'est pas le cas des deux précédents, il n'est nul besoin d'en faire, dans le dictionnaire, une entrée spéciale. Mais, ici encore, le critère sémantique peut être trop difficile à appliquer pour qu'on le préfère au test de non-détermination. Le cas de *corne de l'Afrique* appliqué à la Somalie et aux pays avoisinants illustre bien les situations, qui ne sont pas rares, où, en l'absence d'un critère formel comme celui du non-emploi de l'article devant le second élément, on peut être tenté d'identifier un mot composé jusqu'au moment où l'on rencontre, sous la plume d'un journaliste, *la corne orientale de l'Afrique*, avec une détermination particulière de *corne* qui repose le problème. Cela ne veut pas dire que le critère n'est pas valable, mais que la réaction des usagers de la langue n'est pas uniforme: il y a, pour les uns, «mot composé»; pour les autres, une combinaison libre d'éléments indépendants.

Ce n'est donc pas l'existence de la combinaison en une seule unité d'éléments par ailleurs indépendants qui pourrait nous amener à mettre en doute la validité de la définition d'où nous sommes partis. Ce qui bloque toute possibilité d'adhésion est la constatation que dans l'usage courant qui est fait du terme «mot» celui-ci peut impliquer, non seulement la désignation d'un «être» ou d'une «idée», mais également des modalités diverses qui déterminent cette désignation, voire l'indication des rapports que l'entité en cause entretient, dans l'expérience du locuteur, avec les autres éléments de cette expérience: le latin *rosarum* «des roses» est un «mot», même si l'on peut entendre dire que c'est «le même mot» que *rosa* «la rose» ou *rosis* «aux roses». Or, on y identifie, outre le lexème «rose», une modalité «pluriel» et le connecteur-fonctionnel «génitif» qui indique la nature particulière des rapports qu'entretient en l'occurrence la rose avec le reste de l'expérience. Dans le danois *byernes* «des villes», on trouve, outre le lexème *by-* «ville», une modalité *-er-* de pluriel, une modalité *-ne-* de défini, et un connecteur *-s* de génitif, le tout en un même «mot». Mais, dans l'équivalent espagnol *de las ciudades*, le génitif est marqué par un «mot écrit» distinct, *de*, le défini par *l-* amalgamé avec l'élément *-a-* qui participe au choix du substantif, et un *-s*, rappel de la modalité pluriel explicitée par le *-es* final de *ciudades*. En d'autres termes, nous avons trois «mots écrits» pour ce qui est l'équivalent exact du «mot écrit» unique du danois. Supposons que nous distinguions entre «mot_1» et «mot_2 (écrit)» comme étant deux polysèmes distincts. Allons-nous nous risquer à dire que nous avons un seul «mot_1» dans *de las ciudades* aussi bien que dans *byernes*? Ou ferons-nous valoir que l'antéposition des modalités et du connecteur change complètement les données?

On sait bien, aujourd'hui, pourquoi les éléments «grammaticaux» postposés tendent à s'amalgamer à leur noyau lexical, alors que les mêmes, préposés, se démarquent formellement de lui: la raison en est que l'identité du noyau lexical se manifeste en priorité dans ses éléments initiaux, perçus naturellement tout d'abord et qui, du fait de la redondance inhérente à toute langue, vont suffire à le faire reconnaître, sans qu'aient à intervenir les éléments finaux: dans *dictionnaire, dictionn-* suffit pour identifier la notion et il importe peu que la fin du noyau s'amalgame plus ou moins avec les grammaticaux postposés. Puisque, à l'inverse, le début du noyau est indispensable à son identification, les locuteurs prendront bien garde de préserver ses particularités et ce, notamment, en insérant fréquemment d'autres déterminations, épithétiques, par exemple, entre les grammaticaux et le noyau: *les gros dictionnaires*. Il y a, sans doute, des exceptions à la règle du maintien de l'identité de l'initiale du noyau: on connaît les alternances initiales des langues celtiques et leur parallèle français représenté par les liaisons. Avec modalité antéposée, on peut citer le cas de l'augment grec d'ἔλαβον «je pris», vs λαμβάνω «je prends». Mais elles étonnent assez ceux qui les rencontrent pour la première fois, pour qu'on puisse reconnaître leur caractère marginal.

Allons-nous devoir définir notre «mot_1» comme l'ensemble composé d'un noyau répondant au test de non-détermination de ses modalités éventuelles et de son connecteur, mais seulement pour autant que ces derniers le suivent dans la chaîne du discours, même si nous ne couvrions plus ainsi le cas d'ἔλαβον? Il est peu vraisemblable qu'on s'y résolve. Lorsqu'on a fait l'effort de retrouver, au-delà des différences strictement formelles, l'identité de *byernes* et de *de las ciudades*, il y a des chances pour qu'on recule devant une définition qui fait intervenir des éléments de pure forme, en dernière analyse non pertinents lorsqu'il s'agit d'unités de sens.

Ce qui pourrait induire à donner aux complexes avec lesquels nous venons d'opérer le même statut qu'aux produits de la composition et de la dérivation est la constatation que les modalités qui y sont impliquées ne sont pas plus susceptibles de déterminations particulières que les éléments individuels des composés et dérivés. En linguistique fonctionnelle, les modalités sont très précisément définies comme des monèmes non déterminables. Toutefois, les deux cas sont tout à fait différents: quand j'ajoute à *les roses* une détermination, comme l'épithète *belles*, cette détermination a, comme point d'incidence, *rose-* et non la pluralité des roses, même si l'accord me fait ajouter un *-s* à *belles*. Si maintenant j'ajoute une détermination au dérivé *boutiquier*, *riche*, par exemple, ce n'est pas la boutique qui est affectée, mais l'ensemble *boutiquier*, c'est-à-dire un individu particulier qui possède une boutique. Si j'ajoute *rich* à l'équivalent anglais *shopkeeper*, ce n'est pas le seul noyau *-keeper* qui est ainsi caractérisé, mais, au même titre, le déterminant *shop-* qui renvoie à ce qui est sans doute la source de la richesse.

Le cas du connecteur génitif, dans des complexes comme *rosarum* ou *byernes*, est un peu particulier. On serait tenté, au premier abord, de l'assimiler à celui des modalités: ce serait également un non-déterminable que n'affectent pas les déterminations éventuelles du noyau. Mais on peut se demander si, dans un complexe comme l'allemand *in den Hof*, il n'y a pas détermination de l'accusatif par la préposition *in*, l'accusatif qui marquait la notion centrale de mouvement (lat. *Romam* «à/vers Rome») s'étant vu, au cours de l'évolution de la langue, précisé au moyen d'adverbes spécifiant l'intériorité (*in*) ou le contact (*ad*). En pure synchronie, cependant, on pourrait peut-être faire valoir que la notion d'intériorité est centrale et la distinction entre «mouvement vers» et «présence dans» marginale. En ce qui nous concerne ici, il suffira de rappeler qu'une détermination du noyau n'affecte pas plus le connecteur, qu'il soit ou non déterminable, que les modalités.

Un des éléments du problème, qui n'intervient pas dans la définition du *Larousse*, est le statut prosodique du mot et ceci peut tenir au fait qu'il se pose, en français, de façon très imprécise. Ce que, dans cette langue, on désigne traditionnellement comme l'accent paraît caractériser la finale d'un complexe qui ne se confond nullement avec le «mot_1», c'est-à-dire la désignation d'une entité unique. Au contraire, l'utilisation de traits d'union pour relier ce qu'on peut appeler les enclitiques finaux à leur noyau, dans *dites-le-lui*, par exemple, tendrait à identifier le «mot prosodique» au «mot graphique». Mais si nous laissons de côté le cas un peu marginal du français et opérons plutôt avec le latin, nous constatons, qu'à quelques enclitiques près, il y a une frappante correspondance entre, d'une part, le complexe formé par le noyau lexical et ses annexes grammaticales postposées, et, d'autre part, le segment à l'intérieur duquel joue le conditionnement de la place de l'accent. Les «mots graphiques» séparés de nos textes latins d'aujourd'hui ne font en fait que reproduire visuellement les données de la prosodie qui d'ailleurs ne sont pas en conflit avec celles de la flexion qui réclame que les désinences, comme ce nom l'indique, se trouvent à la finale du «mot». Ce n'est probablement pas un hasard si la notion de mot, latin *uerbum*, angl. *word*, allemand *Wort* se trouve faire un sens à un stade particulier de l'évolution des langues indo-européennes de l'Occident. C'est bien en référence aux données accentuelles qu'il pourrait être le plus recommandable de conserver le terme de «mot» si l'on ne pouvait craindre que la porte soit ainsi entr'ouverte pour perpétuer des emplois mal définis contre lesquels nous tentons ici de mettre en garde. Il serait moins dangereux d'employer, dans tous les cas, le terme d'unité accentuable pour désigner le segment du discours dans lequel peut être définie la position de l'accent. Libre à celui qui décrit le latin de proposer d'appeler «mot» l'unité qui, dans cette langue, ferait coïncider l'unité accentuelle et le noyau lexical accompagné de ses satellites, si d'anciens adverbes n'étaient déjà en voie de devenir des prépositions, c'est-à-dire des connecteurs qui, du fait de leur antéposition, cessent de faire partie des éléments amalgamés du syntagme nominal.

La pratique fonctionnaliste, celle du moins de la *Grammaire fonctionnelle du français*, ne retient le mot qu'en référence au mot graphique, dans les parties de l'ouvrage où l'on traite à part de la forme écrite de la langue. Ailleurs, l'unité significative de départ est le *monème*, c'est-à-dire le signe minimum, le point du discours où coïncident un sens distinct et une différence formelle pour former une unité de sens non analysable en unités de sens plus petites. La différence formelle correspond souvent à un segment distinct, mais elle peut aussi se présenter sous une forme discontinue, comme dans les cas d'accord, par exemple, dans celui du monème pluriel en français avec *les petits animaux* /leptizanimo/ en face de *le petit animal* /ləptitanimal/. Elle peut aussi avoir une forme variable selon les contextes, comme le monème pluriel de l'anglais, dans *cups* /-s/, *ribs* /-z/, *brushes* /-iz/, *oxen* /-ən/, *deer* (zéro), etc. Elle peut être amalgamée avec les signifiants d'autres monèmes, comme le monème pluriel du latin dans *uiri* /-ī/, *uiros* /-ōs/, *uirorum* /-ōrum/, *uiris* /-īs/.

On désigne comme un *synthème* toute combinaison de monèmes qui a exactement le même comportement syntaxique que les monèmes d'une classe donnée, ce qui couvre le dérivé, le composé et les figements, de type *jeune fille, avoir l'air*, par exemple. Les monèmes qui composent un synthème sont dits «conjoints». Les autres sont dits «libres», même s'ils se trouvent reliés à d'autres dans la graphie, voire amalgamés avec ceux-ci. En fait leur liberté est celle des locuteurs qui sont libres de les employer individuellement pour communiquer leur expérience. Celui qui a dit *rosarum* a bien choisi d'employer le génitif et non l'accusatif ou le datif, même s'il serait incapable de préciser où se trouve ce génitif.

Les combinaisons de monèmes du type des participes ont un comportement syntaxique particulier en ce qu'ils «participent» aux compatibilités de diverses classes. On peut les désigner comme des *complexes parasynthématiques*.

Dans l'usage de Saussure, le terme «syntagme» recouvrait ce que nous désignons comme des synthèmes. Une fois ces derniers mis à part, on peut définir le *syntagme* comme l'ensemble formé par un noyau, ses déterminants et, éventuellement, le connecteur qui relie cet ensemble au reste de l'énoncé. La phrase avec son noyau prédicatif est naturellement un syntagme sans connecteur.

Pour accéder au plus près à ce qu'on désigne traditionnellement comme le mot («mot$_1$»), on a été amené à proposer le terme de *syllemme* en référence à un syntagme dont les seuls déterminants sont des modalités, c'est-à-dire des déterminants non déterminables ou, comme on le dit de façon pittoresque, en s'inspirant d'une visualisation syntaxique, des bouts-de-branche. Un syllemme sera donc un noyau accompagné de ses modalités et éventuellement d'un connecteur: dans le syntagme *avec ses très lourdes valises, avec ses … valises* est un syllemme; un syllemme dont le noyau vient en tête correspond très souvent à ce que la tradition désigne comme un mot.

Nous n'avons jusqu'ici posé que le problème de l'identité syntagmatique du «mot». Reste à considérer le problème de son identité sémantique. L'idéal serait naturellement que toute unité de sens ait toujours la même forme et que cette forme soit distincte de celle de toutes les autres unités significatives de la langue. Or, on sait que cet idéal n'est pleinement atteint nulle part. On trouve partout des homonymes, c'est-à-dire une même forme qui correspond à des sens totalement différents.

La communication langagière n'en est pas affectée si les homonymes n'apparaissent jamais dans exactement les mêmes contextes et les mêmes situations. Soit les deux homophones français *tente* et *tante*. On peut, avec un peu d'imagination, fabriquer des contextes où l'on ne saurait lequel des deux il faut comprendre, mais il ne s'agit jamais que de calembours. Les produits de la polysémie sont, au départ, autre chose que des homonymes. Ce n'est pas un hasard si le «mot» *table* désigne aussi bien le meuble autour duquel on s'installe pour prendre ses repas qu'une liste de titres (*TABLE des matières*) ou de formules arithmétiques (*TABLE de multiplication*). Quiconque connaît tous les sens de *table* peut entrevoir les conditions qui ont fait dériver toutes ces significations d'une seule et même valeur primitive. Mais beaucoup d'usagers de la langue ne connaissent la forme que dans des contextes comme *as-tu appris ta table?, nous allons nous mettre à table* qui ne permettent pas à eux seuls de retrouver cette valeur. Il y a donc pour eux deux homonymes *table* qu'ils pourront employer toute leur vie sans jamais s'aviser de les rapprocher.

Le maintien de la polysémie se justifie par les mêmes raisons qu'on invoque pour expliquer la possibilité de l'homonymie: dans les deux cas, les contextes sont différents et préviennent toute ambiguïté. Dans le cas de la polysémie, c'est l'emploi, un peu forcé au départ, de la forme dans un contexte particulier qui a gauchi le sens et c'est la présence de ce contexte qui maintient et finalement accuse la différenciation sémantique.

La chose est si vraie que, dans certains cas, les étymologistes eux-mêmes ne savent si certaines identités formelles sont dues au hasard, avec le secours de ce qu'on appelle l'attraction paronymique — c'est-à-dire le fait d'identifier complètement des formes au départ peu différentes dont l'une est un peu rare — ou si elles résultent d'une expansion polysémique. C'est ce qui se passe, en français, avec *fraise*, avec quatre ou cinq sens différents et plusieurs étymologies douteuses.

Nous ne sommes, bien entendu, jamais obligés de poser ce problème en termes de «mots». Il s'agit, dans tous les cas, de valeurs différentes attribuées à une même forme. Mais, homonymes ou polysèmes, toutes les formes citées ci-dessus sont des monèmes. Seraient-elles des synthèmes, comme *centenaire* (d'un événement) et *centenaire* (un individu), que la situation serait identique: nous aurions affaire non à des syntagmes comportant, outre un noyau, des satellites, mais à des unités syntaxiquement simples. Il n'y a donc aucune raison d'invoquer ici autre chose que le monème, qui est naturellement toujours conçu comme faisant participer à son fonctionnement tous les synthèmes qui entrent dans la même classe que lui.

Non seulement la linguistique fonctionnelle n'apporte aucune réponse à la question de savoir si deux formes identiques sont le même monème ou deux monèmes différents, mais elle enseigne qu'il n'y a, en stricte synchronie, aucune réponse possible. Ce sera à chaque lexicographe de trancher, en faisant, s'il le désire, intervenir l'étymologie, si elle est disponible. Il s'efforcera, là où c'est possible d'ordonner les différentes valeurs de façon que s'impose la possibilité, voire la justification, du passage de l'une à la suivante. Il présentera peut-être tout d'abord une valeur qui n'est plus de celles qui sont synchroniquement attestées, disons, pour *table* «surface plane», si elle permet à l'utilisateur du dictionnaire de ramener à l'unité les valeurs divergentes.

Il y a beaucoup de chances pour que le point de vue qu'il adopte soit plus prescriptif que scientifique, et ceci pose la question d'une description parfaitement objective des usages lexicaux: comment les sujets se comportent-ils réellement en ces matières? et, lorsqu'on dit «les sujets», on ne pense pas nécessairement à des lettrés et à des savants, mais aux mêmes informateurs qui nous ont servi pour dégager la phonologie et la grammaire de leurs usages particuliers. On sait le temps qu'il aura fallu pour qu'on se décide à présenter d'une langue, la prononciation ou, mieux, les prononciations réelles et enregistrables, plutôt que l'idée qu'on se faisait d'une norme. Sans réclamer la mise au point d'un dictionnaire des usages lexicaux réels d'une communauté linguistique, ne pourrait-on envisager la description d'un idiolecte où l'on distinguerait les emplois actifs et les identifications passives, les conditions d'emploi de chaque unité, ce qu'elle suggère précisément? Soit, pour *bouvreuil*, par exemple, l'indication de ce que représente le terme pour la personne en cause; soit 1. ?; 2. «un oiseau»; 3. «un oiseau du type passereau»; 4. «un passereau noir et rouge de taille un peu supérieure à la moyenne», etc. Dans un premier temps, on devrait sans doute se contenter de couvrir un domaine particulier, par exemple, les animaux et les végétaux. Est-ce trop demander que l'on étende à l'étude du lexique — même s'il cesse, dès qu'intervient le sens, d'appartenir au domaine du discret — les principes de la recherche désintéressée? Lorsqu'on est bien convaincu que «désintéressé» ne veut pas dire «irresponsable» et que cette recherche doit se faire au nom d'une pertinence spécifique avec un souci constant de définir précisément les termes dont on se sert, on aura retrouvé les bases réelles de toute recherche scientifique.

Références

Martinet, A. 1960. *Éléments de linguistique générale*. Paris: A. Colin.

Martinet, A. 1965. «Le mot». *Diogène* 48. 39-53. (Repris dans *Problèmes de langage*, 39-53, Paris: Gallimard; trad. anglaise: «The Word», *Diogenes* 51. 38-54).

Martinet, A. et al. 1979. *Grammaire fonctionnelle du français*. Paris: Crédif-Didier.

Martinet, A. 1985. *Syntaxe générale*. Paris: A. Colin.

W. P. SCHMID
(Sprachwissenschaftliches Seminar, Universität Göttingen)

EINE REVIDIERTE SKIZZE EINER ALLGEMEINEN THEORIE DER WORTARTEN*

0. Im Jahre 1970 wurde der Akademie der Wissenschaften und der Literatur zu Mainz eine *Skizze einer allgemeinen Theorie der Wortarten* [im Folgenden kurz *Skizze* genannt], vorgelegt, die den Zweck verfolgte, mit vier auf alle Wortarten einheitlich angewandten Kriterien eine Klassifikation zu erreichen, die ihrerseits sowohl der vor allem in der deutschen Grammatik üblichen, meist semantisch orientierten Kriterienvielfalt, als auch der unbefriedigenden Wortdefinition: «was zwischen zwei Pausen steht», entgegenzutreten versuchte. Darüber hinaus sollte gerade den Sprachhistorikern eine allgemeine Definitionsmöglichkeit in die Hand gegeben werden, die es ihnen erlaubte, z. B. ein Verbum der einen Sprache mit dem Verbausdruck einer anderen Sprache auch dann zu vergleichen, wenn die aus der Antike übernommene, morphologische Definition gar nicht mehr anwendbar ist. Es war klar, daß ein solcher Versuch sich von allen morphologischen Argumenten lösen und auf allgemeine zeichentheoretische Funktionsmerkmale stützen mußte. Das bedeutete aber zugleich, daß man mit der seit de Saussure üblichen Zweigliederung: Bezeichnendes - Bezeichnetes nicht mehr auskommen konnte, sondern außerdem die syntaktische Funktion der Zeichen zu berücksichtigen hatte. Als zweite Neuerung kam hinzu, daß neben der semantischen Funktion (± SEM) und syntaktischen Funktion (± SYN) nun auch die sogenannte pragmatische Funktion (± PRAG) eingeführt wurde, welche alle diejenigen Funktionen des sprachlichen Zeichens umfaßt, die es nicht in Relation zu irgend einem Gegenstand oder Sachverhalt setzen, sondern in Bezug zu Sprecher und Sprechsituation. Gemeint sind damit vor allem diejenigen Zeichen, die beim Wechsel des Sprechers oder bei der Veränderung der Sprechsituation ebenfalls ersetzt

* Die folgenden Ausführungen sind eine Weiterentwicklung von Schmid (1970). Besondere Abweichungen werden genannt. Auf die seitdem erschienene, reiche Literatur zur Zeichentheorie und zu den einzelnen Wortarten kann hier im Einzelnen nicht eingegangen werden.

werden müssen, wie z. B. die Personal- und Demonstrativpronomina, aber auch bestimmte temporale, modale und lokale Ausdrücke. Als viertes Kriterium kam die Entscheidung über die Frage hinzu, ob die Zeichen allein oder nur in Verbindung mit anderen Zeichen einen Satz oder eine Satzkonstituente bilden können (± AUT). Dies implizierte natürlich gewisse Voraussetzungen hinsichtlich der Zahl und der Art der Satzkonstituenten. Für die Frage der Wortartenklassifizierung reichte der Hinweis darauf aus, daß man im Einklang mit der einfachsten Schulgrammatik, aber auch mit der Dependenzgrammatik, der Kasusgrammatik oder auch der generativen Grammatik mit einer Satzkonstituente Adverbiale zu rechnen hat. Auf diese Weise gelangte man dazu, jedem Zeichenträger ein Funktionsmerkmalbündel:

$$Z = [\pm \text{SEM}, \pm \text{SYN}, \pm \text{PRAG}, \pm \text{AUT}]$$

zuzuordnen, wobei die Reihenfolge prinzipiell zwar beliebig, die gegebene mit der Vorausstellung von [± SEM] aus praktischen, aber auch aus theoretischen Gründen vorzuziehen ist. Die sich so ergebenden $2^4 = 16$ Möglichkeiten reichten aus, um die gewünschte Zeichenklassifikation zu erreichen. Eine geringere Zahl von Funktionsmerkmalen würde dieses Ziel verfehlen, eine größere Zahl von Merkmalen, die bei Hinzufügung nur eines weiteren Merkmals bereits 32 verschiedene Zeichensorten erzeugen, würde nicht nur eine Tabelle mit vielen nicht ausgenutzten Möglichkeiten ergeben, sondern auch den Beweis vermissen lassen, daß eine solche Funktion zur Differenzierung von mehr als einer Wortart notwendig wäre. Beispielsweise könnte man sich vorstellen, daß eine Unterscheidung von Substantiv und Eigenname sinnvoll wäre, da sie auch einzelsprachlich eine Reihe syntaktischer Konsequenzen hat. Da es aber keine zweite Wortart gibt, die sich in entsprechender Weise aufgliedern läßt, wird der Eigenname besser als Subkategorie des Substantivums aufgefaßt und damit wie alle anderen Subklassifizierungen aus der vorgelegten Tabelle verbannt.

1. Im Laufe der Zeit wurde die Interpretation der Matrix in einzelnen Punkten gegenüber der veröffentlichten geändert. Darauf einzugehen ist angesichts der im Folgenden vorzunehmenden Revision überflüssig geworden. Den Hauptgrund für eine Neuinterpretation der vorgeschlagenen Matrix lieferte das Kardinalzahlwort, das implizit unter dem Einfluß einiger grammatischer Darstellungen[1] unter dem Adjektiv einge-

[1] Vgl. *Dudengrammatik* (§ 527; 1532ff.); *Grundzüge einer deutschen Grammatik* (1981: 495, 607).

ordnet worden war, obwohl es im Gegensatz zum Ordinale in den verschiedenen indogermanischen und auch nicht-indogermanischen Sprachen soviele Besonderheiten aufweist, daß eine Unterordnung unter die Wortart Adjektiv zu erheblichen Schwierigkeiten führt. Bemerkenswerterweise hat schon G. Frege das Kardinale scharf vom Adjektiv getrennt (Frege 1884: 58). Die historisch-etymologische Untersuchung der Zahlwortreihe: eins, zwei, drei ... führt zu einem Gemisch aus Pronomina, Adjektiven und Substantiven, in Einzelfällen zu überhaupt keinem Ergebnis (etwa bei fünf und sechs). Die Notwendigkeit einer Trennung des Kardinale von den Adjektiven ergibt sich aber auch unabhängig von mathematisch-philosophischen Überlegungen aus folgenden linguistischen Argumenten:

1) Die Kardinalzahlwörter nehmen vielfach eine andere Stellung im Satz ein als die Adjektiva. So geht z. B. im Lateinischen das Zahlwort in der Regel dem Substantiv voraus, während das Adjektiv ihm folgt[2]. Noch deutlicher wird das im Neupersischen, wo das Adjektiv mit Hilfe der *Iżafet*-Konstruktion dem Substantiv angehängt wird, während das Zahlwort ohne besondere Kennzeichnung dem Substantiv vorangestellt wird[3].

2) Während Ausdrücke wie «fleissige Schüler» aus der prädikativen Stellung hergeleitet werden können oder bei sekundären Adjektiven wie «die serbische Fichte» aus präpositionalen Verbindungen wie «die Fichte ist aus Serbien», ist eine solche Transformation bei den Kardinalzahlen nicht möglich.

3) In den Sprachen, die beim Adjektiv Deklinationsendungen bewahren, tendieren die Kardinale zur Flexionslosigkeit[4].

4) Im Germanischen, Baltischen und Slavischen, denen eine doppelte Adjektivflexion eigen ist, haben die Kardinalia keinen Anteil an dieser Unterscheidungsmöglichkeit.

5) Die Kardinalia können nur mit sich selbst, nicht aber mit dem attributiven Adjektiv durch «und» verbunden werden. Dies müßte der Fall sein, wenn die Kardinalia Adjektiva wären.

6) Kardinalia können bestimmte Kasusformen des Substantivs regieren (z. B. im Russischen, das *odin, odna, odno* «ein(s)» adjektivisch konstruiert, *dva, tri, četyre* «zwei, drei, vier» mit dem Substantiv im Genitiv

[2] Vgl. Szantyr (1965: 406, 408) mit weiteren Einzelheiten und Abweichungen.

[3] Salemann - Shukovski (1947: § 21, § 26d); Lazard (1963: 201, 217ff.) mit Ausnahmen, die dem Lateinischen vergleichbar sind.

[4] Eine Ausnahme macht das Lettische, das die Zahlen 1-10 adjektivisch dekliniert. Vgl. aber Punkt 4.

Sing. und ab *pjat'* «fünf» das Substantiv im Genitiv Plur. verbindet und einen Satz wie *ėti dva poslednich pacienta prichodit* «diese (Nom. Plur.)-zwei (Nom.)-letzten (Gen. Plur.)-Patienten (Gen. Sing.)-kommen (3. Pers. Sing.)» als grammatisch akzeptiert (vgl. Comrie 1981: 101-104).
7) Kardinalia sind im Gegensatz zu den primären Adjektiven nicht steigerungsfähig. Sie spielen die Rolle von definiten Plurativa zu den Indefinitpronomina und können durch Substantivierung zu Kollektiva werden, die dann mit *Mehrheit, Vielheit* etc. auf einer Stufe stehen.
8) Kardinalia können in ihrer Klasse nur zu Dvandva-Komposita führen, während die Adjektiva auch Determinativkomposita bilden können.
9) Aus (8) ergibt sich, daß sich Adjektiva in semantische Felder ordnen lassen. Die Kardinalia können nur Reihen bilden.
10) Im Falle, daß die Bezeichnung des gezählten Gegenstandes das Merkmal [-zählbar] trägt, treten Zählwörter auf (deutlicher noch im Chinesischen und Japanischen), die dann Unterscheidungen wie *Holz* [-zählbar], *drei Hölzer* (= drei Holzarten), *drei Stück Holz* ermöglichen[5].

Aus diesen zehn Punkten geht mit wünschenswerter Deutlichkeit hervor, daß es ganz unmöglich ist, in einem übereinzelsprachlichen Klassifikationsversuch die Kardinalzahlwörter als eine Unterklasse der Adjektiva zu betrachten, m. a. W., die Kardinalia bilden eine eigene Klasse im System der Wortarten, die — wie hier nicht weiter ausgeführt werden kann — zu anderen Wortarten eigene Beziehungen unterhält.

Wenn dieses Ergebnis richtig ist, dann bedarf unsere eingangs erwähnte *Skizze* einer gründlichen Korrektur, denn es muß für die Kardinalia ein Platz geschaffen werden, ohne daß sich die Gesamtzahl der Wortarten ändert, d. h. die Matrix bleibt konstant, ihre Interpretation wird geändert. Das läßt sich dadurch erreichen, daß man das Funktionsmerkmal «Syntaktisch» [± SYN] etwas schärfer faßt.

Das Merkmal [+ SYN] soll nur denjenigen Wortarten zugeschrieben werden, die innerhalb einer Satzkonstituente andere Wortarten oder darüber hinaus sogar andere Satzkonstituenten regieren, während [− SYN] auf Wortarten bezogen wird, die regiert werden.
Auf einige Konsequenzen, die diese Neubestimmung in sich birgt, muß bei der Besprechung der einzelnen Wortarten eingegangen werden.

Damit können wir die vier verschiedenen Zeichenfunktionen wie folgt umschreiben:

[5] Zur Form und Geschichte des Ausdrucks vom Typ «drei Glas Bier» vgl. Paul (1919: § 185); Behaghel (1923: 531 ff., 541).

[+ SEM]: Das Zeichen bezieht sich auf Lebewesen, Gegenstände oder Sachverhalte, bzw. Klassen von ihnen. Die Bedeutungen sind im Lexikon angebbar.

[− SEM]: Das Zeichen hat keine eigene Bedeutung im Sinne von [+ SEM], kann aber eine solche aus dem jeweiligen Text- oder Situationszusammenhang erhalten.

[+ SYN]: Das Zeichen übt einen Einfluß auf andere Zeichen (u. U. mit morphologisch verändernder Wirkung) aus, es regiert.

[− SYN]: Das Zeichen wird regiert, kann aber aus Transformationen sekundär syntaktische Eigenschaften annehmen, die ihm seiner Art nach eigentlich nicht zukommen.

[+ PRAG]: Das Zeichen gibt den Bezug zum Sprecher oder zur Sprechsituation an. Gemeint sind damit Beziehungen zum Sprecher, Angesprochenen, Besprochenen, die verschiedenen Arten der Deixis, der temporalen, lokalen und modalen Beziehungen, sofern sie sprecherbezogen und nicht lexikalisiert sind. Nicht gemeint ist damit K. Bühlers Ausdrucksfunktion der Zeichen und auch nicht G. Hammarströms β-Ebene (s. *Skizze* S. 8).

[− PRAG]: Das Zeichen hat keinen ihm eigenen Bezug zur Sprechsituation, kann aber solche aus bestimmten Sprechsituationen übernehmen.

[+ AUT]: Das Zeichen kann allein eine Satzkonstituente bilden.

[− AUT]: Das Zeichen kann nur in Kombination mit anderen Zeichen eine Satzkonstituente bilden[6].

Eine Kombination aus diesen vier jeweils positiv oder negativ spezifizierten Funktionsmerkmalen der kleinst möglichen Lautfolge einer Äußerung als Zeichenträger zugeordnet nennen wir Wort einer natürlichen Sprache[7].

Aus den negativ spezifizierten, bzw. nicht markierten Merkmalen ergibt sich schon hier, daß wir bei den verschiedenen Wortarten sowohl mit Neutralisierungen einzelner Merkmale als auch mit Vererbung von Merkmalen aus dem Kontext im weitesten Sinne des Wortes rechnen müssen.

2. Aus rein praktischen, mnemotechnischen Gründen empfiehlt es sich, statt der « ± » Zeichen die Kennzeichnung durch 1/0 vorzunehmen. In

[6] Zum Problem der Autonomie vgl. François (1970).

[7] Man beachte die Abweichung gegenüber der von Bloomfield (1926: 156). Vgl. auch Marchand (1969: 1 mit Anm. 1).

der folgenden Tabelle wird also «1» mit «+» und «0» mit «−» identifiziert. So ergeben sich folgende Variationen:

	± SEM	± SYN	± PRAG	± AUT
I.	1	1	1	1
II.	1	1	1	0
III.	1	1	0	1
IV.	1	1	0	0
V.	1	0	1	1
VI.	1	0	1	0
VII.	1	0	0	1
VIII.	1	0	0	0
IX.	0	1	1	1
X.	0	1	1	0
XI.	0	1	0	1
XII.	0	1	0	0
XIII.	0	0	1	1
XIV.	0	0	1	0
XV.	0	0	0	1
XVI.	0	0	0	0

3. Wenigstens für den Kreis der indogermanischen Sprachen kann man nun eine Zuordnung dieser Variationen zu je einer Wortart vornehmen, so daß bei einer Übertragung von Begriffen wie Substantiv, Verbum, Adverb, Adjektiv auf andere, auch nicht-indogermanische Sprachen die ihnen jeweils zugeordneten Funktionsmerkmale gegeben sein müssen. Wir gelangen also zu folgenden Interpretationen:

I. **1 1 1 1** = [+ SEM, + SYN, + PRAG, + AUT] entspricht der Wortart *finites Verbum*. Beispiel: lat. *dixi*. Die semantische Funktion wird durch das Morphem **deik̂-*, die syntaktische Funktion durch die Rektion (*case frame*), die pragmatische Funktion durch Tempussuffix und Personalendung zum Ausdruck gebracht. Die Autonomie ergibt sich aus der Tatsache, daß *dixi* allein eine Satzkonstituente, ja sogar einen Satz bilden kann. Werden die vier Funktionen nicht in einem Wort ausgedrückt wie in vielen modernen Sprachen, kann man also erst dann von einem finiten Verbum sprechen, wenn durch das obligatorische Hinzutreten anderer Wortarten die Funktionsbedingungen erfüllt werden, so daß **1 1 1 1** gar nicht mehr durch ein Wort, sondern durch einen Wortkomplex zum Ausdruck kommt. Zugleich ergibt sich daraus, daß das, was gewöhnlich in einem Verbparadigma zusammengefaßt wird, aus ganz unterschiedlichen Wortarten (finite Verben, Infinitive, Partizipien) besteht. Pointiert gesagt heißt das, daß der nicht spezifizierte Begriff *Verbum* entweder nur ein Lexem oder ein Wortkomplex oder ein Paradigma, aber keine Wortart ist. Eine einheitliche Definition des Verbums, die das gesamte Paradigma umfaßt, gibt es nicht. Anzumerken wäre noch, daß auch vom morphologischen Standpunkt aus betrachtet infinite Formen (Partizipien, Infinitive) die Funktion finiter Verben annehmen können wie z. B. die russischen Praeterita, das altindische Futurum in der 3. Person Sing. oder die Ausdrucksweise des Nominalstils im klassischen Sanskrit. Da die vorliegende Klassifizierung unabhängig von der Morphologie ist, entsteht dadurch kein Widerspruch.

II. **1 1 1 0** = [+ SEM, + SYN, + PRAG, − AUT] entspricht dem *finiten Hilfsverbum* (vgl. Palmer 1979). Beispiel: *dictum EST, dictum HABEO*, deutsch: *ich HABE gesagt, ich WERDE sagen* u. a. Finite Hilfsverben sind also dadurch charakterisiert, daß sie stets mit anderen Wortarten eine obligatorische Verbindung eingehen, nie selbständig auftreten. Sie tragen aber stets einen Teil der semantischen, vor allem aber die syntaktische und pragmatische Funktion. Treten Verben wie *sein, haben, werden* oder englisch *to do* selbständig auf z. B. als Existenz-, Besitz- oder Vorgangs-Verbum, gehören sie zur Klasse I, falls es sich nicht um aus dem Kontext zu ergänzende Ellipsen handelt.

III. **1 1 0 1** = [+ SEM, + SYN, − PRAG, + AUT] entspricht der Wortart *Substantiv*. Man sieht, daß diese Wortart nicht — wie es gern, vor allem in der inhaltbezogenen Grammatik, aber zu Unrecht geschieht — durch semantische Differenzen von der Wortart finites Verbum getrennt wird, sondern allein durch das Fehlen der pragmatischen Komponente. In der Tat zeigen ja Substantiva wie *dictio, dictator* dasselbe Lexem wie *dixi*. Der Satz: *Die Sonne geht auf* und das Substantiv *Sonnenaufgang* lassen sich zwar semantisch gleichsetzen, aber nicht pragmatisch. Man beachte, daß erst durch die Vernachlässigung der pragmatischen Komponente in der Government and Binding-Theory Chomskys *John proved the theorem* and *John's proof of the theorem* ein und derselben Struktur zugewiesen werden können. Die Nominalisierung des finiten Verbums erfolgt also durch Streichung der pragmatischen Funktion (also durch den Verzicht auf den Bezug zu Sprecher und

Sprechsituation), was für das Auffinden der pragmatischen Elemente wesentlich ist. Dabei kann es in den Einzelsprachen sehr wohl vorkommen, daß Infinitive und Verbalsubstantive von verschiedenen Tempusstämmen aus gebildet werden. Daraus ergibt sich, daß dann die an sich pragmatische Kategorie Tempus teilweise lexikalisiert worden ist. — Die Autonomie folgt daraus, daß Substantiva allein einen Satzteil bilden können. Das Merkmal [+ SYN] spiegelt die Tatsache wider, daß das Substantiv andere Wortarten (z. B. wiederum das Substantiv oder das Adjektiv) regiert und in Subjekt-Stellung auch Einfluß auf das Prädikat haben kann. In anderen Stellungen, z. B. als Objekt, als Attribut oder als Adverbiale wird das Merkmal [+ SYN] neutralisiert. Das bedeutet, daß das Substantiv in unterschiedlichen Relationen zum finiten Verbum stehen kann, die man mit Zuordnung (Subjekt), Unterordnung (Objekt) und Beiordnung (Adverbiale) bezeichnen könnte. Das Verkettungssymbol « + » in früheren Versionen der Chomsky-Grammatik reicht daher nicht aus, diesen Abhängigkeitsverhältnissen Rechnung zu tragen. Richtig ist, daß man heute in den unterschiedlichen Grammatiktheorien geneigt ist, der Subjekt-Stellung eine Sonderrolle zuzuweisen, aber das geschah bereits auch in traditionellen, historischen Grammatiken, die sich auf besondere Ablautformen des Nominativs berufen konnten.

IV. **1 1 0 0** = [+ SEM, + SYN, − PRAG, − AUT]. In Korrektur unserer *Skizze* (S. 11ff.) interpretieren wir jetzt diese Variation mit dem *Kardinalzahlwort* und entnehmen die Begründung dafür den in Abschnitt 1 vorgebrachten Argumenten. Am wichtigsten ist dabei vielleicht die Charakterisierung durch [− AUT]. Das bedeutet nämlich, daß vom sprachlichen Standpunkt aus gesehen, das Kardinale primär ein Zählwort ist, also immer einer Ergänzung durch ein Substantiv bedarf. Die Verwendung in arithmetischen oder zahlentheoretischen Sätzen, die Aussagen über Zahlen oder eine bestimmte Zahl machen, impliziert stets eine Substantivierung des Zahlworts[8]. Aus der Substantivierbarkeit folgt auch die positive Markierung der semantischen Funktion. Aus Punkt (6) und (10) ergibt sich [+ SYN], aus der Unabhängigkeit von der Sprechsituation, d. h. der Objektivierbarkeit aller Zahlenangaben ergibt sich [− PRAG]. Das Kardinalzahlwort kann nun jedoch nicht nur substantiviert werden, es kann auch adjektiviert werden in Gestalt des Ordinalzahlworts. Daß in der Adjektivierung nicht nur syntaktische, sondern auch pragmatische Unterschiede zur Geltung kommen, läßt sich an

[8] Über den Zahlbegriff vgl. Frege (1884); Scriba (1968); Hammerich (1966); Artmann (1983: 176ff.).

einem einfachen Beispiel verdeutlichen. Darüber, daß fünf Bücher auf einem Tisch liegen, werden sich alle diejenigen, die an dem Tisch sitzen, schnell einigen. Welches der Bücher aber als das fünfte gelten soll, bedarf einer situationsgebundenen Absprache.

V. **1 0 1 1** = [+ SEM, − SYN, + PRAG, + AUT] entspricht der Wortart *Adverb*, sofern es sich dabei nicht um präpositionale Verbindungen, um pronominale Adverbien oder um Partikeln handelt (s. Nr. XIII, XIV). Die Morphologie der Adverbien in den Einzelsprachen zeigt, daß sie stets mit Suffixen (mit Einschluß des ø-Morphems) gebildet werden, die die Abhängigkeit von den Kasusbeziehungen zum Verbum aufheben (vgl. lat. *maxime, libenter*). Selbst wenn das Adverb mit zum Kasussystem gehörigen Endungen ausgestattet ist, werden diese in der Stellung des Adverbiale neutralisiert und nehmen dann nicht mehr an der Flexion teil. So ist lat. *universus* als Adverb synchron kein Nominativ, *partim* kein Akkusativ, *cito* kein Ablativ mehr. Das Satzadverb ist dem Verbum beigeordnet und deswegen in seiner Stellung freier als die in zuordnender oder unterordnender Funktion auftretenden Satzkonstituenten. Es kann hier nur angedeutet werden, daß sich aus der relativ freien Adverbialstellung nähere Bestimmungen aller übrigen Satzkonstituenten ableiten lassen, wobei die nähere Bestimmung des Verbums nur eine von mehreren Möglichkeiten ist. Vgl.

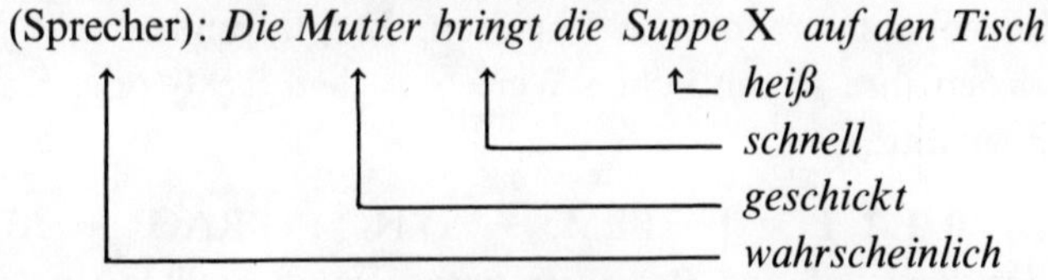

VI. **1 0 1 0** = [+ SEM, − SYN, + PRAG, − AUT] wird in Abweichung von *Skizze* S. 11 als *Adjektiv* interpretiert. Beispiel: lat. *dicax, dicens, dictus*. Die Begründung dafür ist praktisch mit der in Abschnitt 1 ausgeführten Gegenüberstellung mit dem Zahlwort mitgeliefert worden (vgl. auch IV). Das Adjektiv ist abhängig [− AUT] entweder vom Hilfsverbum (II) oder vom Substantiv (III) und ist stets in seiner Form fremdbestimmt [− SYN]. Es enthält besonders dann, wenn es gesteigert wird, eine pragmatische Komponente, die man nicht erst — wie noch in *Skizze* S. 12 versucht — als Vererbung aus der prädikativen Stellung herleiten muß[9]. Dagegen wird man nicht umhin können, eine

[9] Vgl. schon Bierwischs (1967) Merkmal [+ Observe]; anders *Skizze*, S. 12.

solche Erklärung für die Fälle zu Hilfe zu nehmen, in denen vom attributiven Adjektiv wieder bestimmte Kasus abhängig sind («*gleich*» + Dat., «*ähnlich*» + Dat., «*teilhaftig*» + Gen. etc.). Besonders deutlich wird das bei den Partizipien, die als Adjektivierung des finiten Verbums verstanden werden, und aus dieser Wortart bestimmte Kasusrektionen und Adverbverbindungen mitbringen.

VII. **1 0 0 1** = [+ SEM, − SYN, − PRAG, + AUT] ist den lexikalisierten *Onomatopoetika* zuzuschreiben[10], die in fast jeder Satzkonstituente unverändert auftreten können, und daher ihre syntaktische Bestimmung stets von den anderen Wortarten erhalten. Ein reiches Material für diese Wortart liefert das Litauische[11].

VIII. **1 0 0 0** = [+ SEM, − SYN, − PRAG, − AUT] entspricht den lexikalisierten *Interjektionen*, die in der Regel außerhalb des syntagmatischen Zusammenhangs im Satz vorkommen, gelegentlich in Analogie zu anderen Verbindungen jedoch bestimmte Kasusrektionen haben können (*vae victis*). Man könnte daran denken einige von ihnen auch der Klasse XIV (**0 0 1 0**) zuzuordnen. Hinzugefügt sei, daß auch der Vokativ der Substantiva, dessen Form als Nicht-Kasus allen anderen Kasus gegenübersteht (Schmid 1972: 17), in diese Klasse einzugliedern ist.

Die bisher aufgezählten Wortarten I-VIII haben alle eine im Lexikon angebbare semantische Funktion. Die folgenden acht Wortarten beziehen ihre semantischen Werte aus dem Text- oder Situationszusammenhang.

IX. **0 1 1 1** = [− SEM, + SYN, + PRAG, + AUT] entspricht den *Personal-* und *Demonstrativpronomina*. Sie können wie die Substantiva allein eine Satzkonstituente bilden, sind in der Art ihrer Deixis sprecherbezogen (Schmid 1972: 9ff.). Im Gegensatz zu der in meiner Pragmatischen Komponente gegebenen Darstellung scheint es jedoch empfehlenswert, das Pronomen der 3. Person nicht als neutralisiertes Demonstrativum aufzufassen, sondern es der Wortart XI zuzuordnen[12].

X. **0 1 1 0** = [− SEM, + SYN, + PRAG, − AUT] scheint mehrere traditionelle Wortarten zu umfassen, denn sowohl der *Artikel* als auch das *Possessivum* (vgl. Seiler 1973, 1983) erfüllen die durch die Matrix vorgegebenen Bedingungen. Beide können nicht allein eine Satzkonsti-

[10] Zur Bildungsweise vgl. Wissemann (1954); Hoffmann (1952).
[11] Leskien (1902/3); *Lietuvių kalbos gramatika* II (1971: 715ff., 734-746).
[12] Vgl. darüber Beifuss - Czepluch - Tuschinsky - Schmid (1985).

tuente bilden, sondern richten sich in ihrer Form nach dem übergeordneten Substantiv. Man sollte daher meinen, sie müßten mit [− SYN] ausgezeichnet werden. Dagegen sprechen jedoch diejenigen Sprachen, die eine doppelte Adjektivflexion kennen. In diesen Sprachen entscheidet — soweit vorhanden — der Artikel oder das Possessivum über die Wahl der Adjektivform. Definitionsgemäß muß deshalb [+ SYN] eingesetzt werden. Allerdings ist hinzuzufügen, daß der Artikel nicht in allen indogermanischen Sprachen als eigene Wortart vorkommt und daß auch die Rektion des Possessivums einzelsprachlich abweicht. Griechisch, Deutsch, Litauisch und Lettisch zeigen hier beträchtliche Unterschiede, die weiterer Untersuchung bedürfen. Wenn man sich darüber einig ist, daß der bestimmte Artikel eine determinierende, in die Sprechsituation einbeziehende Funktion hat, dann muß man einräumen, daß er nicht gleichzeitig eine generalisierende Funktion haben kann, wie in manchen grammatischen Darstellungen behauptet wird. Tatsächlich aber wird die Generalisierung durch Pluralbildung und Fehlen des Artikels zum Ausdruck gebracht (*Igel sind Stacheltiere*), eine definitorische Einführung durch den Singular mit unbestimmtem Artikel (*ein Igel ist ein Stacheltier*) erreicht, während *der Igel ist ein Stacheltier* immer schon ein Vorverständnis des Igel-Begriffes voraussetzt. Der bestimmte Artikel hat also pragmatische Funktion, unter welche sich seine determinierenden, definierenden, identifizierenden, klassifizierenden, individualisierenden, konkretisierenden und wie auch immer genannten Funktionen subsumieren lassen.

XI. **0 1 0 1** = [− SEM, + SYN, − PRAG, + AUT] läßt sich ähnlich dem Artikel (X) auch historisch aus der Wortart IX herleiten. Es handelt sich um das *Pronomen der 3. Person*, in welchem die deiktische (meist jener-deiktische) Funktion gegen null tendiert. In diese Klasse gehören auch die *Relativa* und *Fragepronomina*. Sie alle verweisen auf oder fragen nach einem semantischen Objekt, können deswegen in allen nicht-verbalen Satzkonstituenten auftreten und diese selbst bilden, wobei Relativa und Fragepronomina häufig ein und dieselbe Quelle haben[13]. Eine Unterklasse dieser Wortart wird man mit anders gearteter pragmatischer Relation in den Indefinitpronomina zu sehen haben.

XII. **0 1 0 0** = [− SEM, + SYN, − PRAG, − AUT] umfaßt *Konjunktionen, Prä-* und *Postpositionen* samt *Präverbien*. Sie alle bilden keine eigene Satzkonstituente, empfangen ihre semantische oder pragma-

[13] Auch hier gibt es eine Abweichung gegenüber *Skizze*, S. 14.

tische Funktion aus den Sätzen oder Wörtern, die sie verbinden, denen sie vorausgehen oder folgen und deren Syntax sie in Wortstellung oder Kasusrektion beeinflussen. Vom Standpunkt der Sprachgeschichte sind sie oft aus Adverbien (**1 0 1 1**) hervorgegangen, indem sie ihre semantische und syntaktische Eigenständigkeit aufgegeben haben. Dabei wurde zugleich das syntaktische Verhältnis umgekehrt. Während die Adverbien zunächst auch zur semantischen Spezifizierung mehrdeutiger Kasusbeziehungen dienten, dient die Präposition u. U. als Kasusanzeiger und erhält ihre semantische Funktion (temporal, lokal, modal) von den Substantiven, die sie regiert. — In Abweichung von meiner früheren Darstellung wird man in diese Klasse auch die Satznegationen (lat. *non, ne,* altind. *mā*) zu stellen haben, die in einigen Sprachen syntaktische Konsequenzen haben (Altindisch, Avestisch, Griechisch, Lateinisch) oder entwickeln (in den slavischen Sprachen). Die teilweise vorhandene pragmatische Komponente der Modalität ergibt sich aus dem von ihnen verlangten Modus. Wortnegationen und Modalitätspartikel (wie griech. ἄν, κε(ν)) wird man eher der Wortart XIV zuweisen.

XIII. **0 0 1 1** = [− SEM, − SYN, + PRAG, + AUT] entspricht der Klasse der sogenannten *Proadverbien*, wie lat. *hīc, nunc,* deutsch *heute, jetzt, bald, dann*, die wie die Adverbien eine eigene Satzkonstituente, das Adverbiale, bilden, aber ihre Semantik aus ihrem Bezug zur Sprechsituation beziehen.

XIV. **0 0 1 0** = [− SEM, − SYN, + PRAG, − AUT] umfaßt wiederum mehrere traditionell verschiedene Wortarten, nämlich *Hervorhebungs-, Negations-* und *Modalitätspartikel* sowie *Wortadverbien* wie lat. *magis*, deutsch *sehr, besonders, zu.*

XV. **0 0 0 1** = [− SEM, − SYN, − PRAG, + AUT] meint die *Satzpause.*

XVI. **0 0 0 0** = [− SEM, − SYN, − PRAG, − AUT] meint die *Wortpause.*

Die Auffassung der Pausen als Wörter, möglicherweise vergleichbar mit dem Wort der Länge Null in formalen Sprachen, ist nicht nur eine Folge des Zuordnungszwanges zu unserer Matrix, sondern bietet interessante Perspektiven für das bedeutungsvolle Schweigen (vgl. Guardini 1983: 51ff.). Auf der anderen Seite werden dadurch Wortdefinitionen mit Hilfe der Pausen zirkulär, da nicht nur ein Wort zwischen zwei Pausen, sondern auch eine Pause zwischen zwei Wörtern steht. In jedem Falle wird der Satz zu einer wie auch immer strukturierten Folge von

Wörtern, die in ihrer Summe wieder [+ SEM, + SYN, + PRAG, + AUT] ergeben müssen. Die Unterscheidung von Wort- und Satzpausen ist nicht nur wegen ihrer unterschiedlichen Verlängerbarkeit notwendig, sondern wird auch durch die altindischen Sandhiregeln, für welche diese Unterscheidung wesentlich ist, nahegelegt.

4. Aus der in Abschnitt 3 versuchten Zuordnung zu den 16 Möglichkeiten der Variation der vier Zeichenfunktionen lassen sich eine Reihe von Konsequenzen ableiten.
1) Eine Klassifikation der Wortarten mit vier durchgehend angewandten Kriterien ist möglich.
2) Es gibt keine eineindeutige Zuordnung, da sowohl einer traditionellen Wortart mehrere Zeilen der Matrix, als auch einer Matrixzeile mehrere traditionelle Wortarten zugeordnet werden. Wegen der Unterschiedlichkeit der jeweils benutzten Kriterien ist das auch gar nicht verwunderlich.
3) Die traditionellen Wortarten erzwingen keinerlei zusätzliches Kriterium. Die Verminderung um ein Kriterium würde die Wortarten nicht umfassen können.
4) Die Wortartentabelle ermöglicht den übereinzelsprachlichen Vergleich und verdeutlicht zugleich, daß auf der einen Seite nicht jede Sprache alle aufgezählten Wortarten besitzen muß (z. B. Artikel), und auf der anderen Seite die Zuordnung im Laufe der Zeit sich auch ändern kann (vgl. Präpositionen).
5) Da es keinen Satz ohne Sprecherbezogenheit geben kann, wird man versuchen, wissenschaftliche, allgemeine Aussagen, mathematische Sätze, theologische Wahrheiten etc. mit einer minimalen pragmatischen Komponente, poetische Sätze mit einer maximalen pragmatischen Komponente zu formulieren.
6) Die vorgeschlagene Klassifizierung will und kann nicht allen historisch gewachsenen Feinheiten der Einzelsprachen gerecht werden. Deren Untersuchung muß zunächst zu Subklassifizierungen, dann aber auch zu Modifikationen der revidierten Skizze führen.
7) Es ist selbstverständlich, daß die hier vorgelegte Klassifizierung, die in erster Linie dem Sprachvergleich einheitliche Kriterien in die Hand geben und von nur intuitiver Übertragung von Wortarten auf andere Sprachen wegführen will, die Bedürfnisse einer maschinellen Textanalyse (Bergenholtz - Schaeder 1977) nicht erfüllen kann. Dennoch bin ich überzeugt, daß die augenblickliche Inkompatibilität nicht grundsätzlicher Art sein muß, sondern durch weitere einzelsprachliche Subklassifizierungen überwunden werden kann.

8) So gewiß es auch ist, daß die jüngste Entwicklung der Chomsky-Grammatik, die Government and Binding Theory mit ihren lexikalischen Kategorien [αN, βV], die zu Substantiv, Verb, Adjektiv und Präposition führen, wegen der Vieldeutigkeit von [-N, -V] eine Fülle von Wortarten undefiniert läßt und Annahmen machen muß, die jeder Sprachgeschichte zuwider laufen, so sicher ist es auch, daß gewisse Ansätze zur Konfigurationalität der Sprachen, zur «move α»-Transformation und zum Kasusverständnis Grundlage einer fruchtbaren allgemeinsprachwissenschaftlichen Auseinandersetzung bilden könnten, sofern sich nur die erforderliche Gesprächsbereitschaft und damit eine Öffnung der fachsprachlichen Terminologie einstellt.

Literatur

Artmann, B. 1983. *Der Zahlbegriff.* Göttingen: Vandenhoeck & Ruprecht.

Behaghel, O. 1923. *Deutsche Syntax. Eine geschichtliche Darstellung I.* Heidelberg: C. Winter.

Beifuss, K. - H. Czepluch - J. Tuschinsky - W.P. Schmid. 1985. «Zur Klassifikation pragmatischer Elemente in der grammatischen Beschreibung». *Sprachwissenschaft* 10. 81-106.

Bergenholtz, H. - B. Schaeder, 1977. *Die Wortarten im Deutschen.* Stuttgart: Klett Verlag.

Bierwisch, M. 1967. «Some semantic universals of German adverbials». *Foundations of Language* 3. 1-36.

Bloomfield, L. 1926. «A set of postulates for the science of language». *Language* 2. 153-164.

Comrie, B. 1981. *Language universals and linguistic typology.* Oxford: Blackwell.

Dudengrammatik der deutschen Gegenwartssprache bearbeitet von P. Grebe. 1973^3. (= Der Große Duden, Bd. 4). Mannheim-Wien-Zürich: Bibliographisches Institut-Dudenverlag.

François, F. 1970. «De l'autonomie fonctionnelle». *La Linguistique* 6. 5-21.

Frege, G. 1884. *Die Grundlagen der Arithmetik.* (Neuausgabe Hildesheim-New York: G. Olms, 1977).

Grundzüge einer deutschen Grammatik, von einem Autorenkollektiv unter der Leitung von K.E. Heidolph, W. Flämig, W. Motsch. 1981. Berlin: Akademieverlag.

Guardini, R. 1983. «Die religiöse Sprache». M. Kaempfert ed., *Probleme der religiösen Sprache*, 50-71. Darmstadt: Wissenschaftliche Buchgesellschaft.

Hammerich, L. 1966. *Zahlwort und Zahlbegriff.* Mannheim: Bibliographisches Institut-Dudenverlag.

Hoffmann, K. 1952. «Wiederholende Onomapoetika im Altindischen». *Indogermanische Forschungen* 60. 254-264 [= *Aufsätze zur Indoiranistik* I, 34-45. Wiesbaden: L. Reichert Verlag, 1975].

Lazard, G. 1963. *La langue des plus anciens monuments de la prose persane.* Paris: Klincksieck.

Leskien, A. 1902-1903. «Schallnachahmungen und Schallverba im Litauischen». *Indogermanische Forschungen* 13. 165-212.

Lietuvių kalbos gramatika II. 1971. Vilnius: Leidykla «Mintis».

Marchand, H. 1969². *The categories and types of present-day English word-formation*. München: C.H. Beck.

Palmer, F.R. 1979. «Why auxiliaries are not main verbs». *Lingua* 47. 1-25.

Paul, H. 1919. *Deutsche Grammatik*. Halle: M. Niemeyer.

Salemann, C. - V. Shukovski. 1947⁴. *Persische Grammatik*. Leipzig: O. Harrassowitz.

Schmid, W.P. 1970. *Skizze einer allgemeinen Theorie der Wortarten* (Abhandlungen der Akademie der Wissenschaften und der Literatur zu Mainz, Geistes- und sozialwissenschaftliche Klasse 1970, 5). Wiesbaden: F. Steiner Verlag.

Schmid, W.P. 1972. *Die Pragmatische Komponente in der Grammatik* (Abhandlungen der Akademie der Wissenschaften und der Literatur zu Mainz, Geistes- und sozialwissenschaftliche Klasse 1972, 9). Wiesbaden: F. Steiner Verlag. [= G. Rauh ed. 1983, *Essays on Deixis*, 61-78. Tübingen: G. Narr].

Scriba, Ch.J. 1968. *The concept of number*. Mannheim-Zürich: Bibliographisches Institut.

Seiler, H. 1973. «Zum Problem der sprachlichen Possessivität». *Folia Linguistica* 6. 231-250.

Seiler, H. 1983. *Possession as an operational dimension of language*. Tübingen: G. Narr.

Szantyr, A. 1965. *Lateinische Syntax und Stilistik* (Handbuch der Altertumswissenschaft II, 2/2). München: C.H. Beck.

Wissemann, H. 1954. *Untersuchungen zur Onomatopoiie*. Heidelberg: C. Winter.

P. SWIGGERS - W. VAN HOECKE
(F.N.R.S. belge) *(K.U. Leuven)*

BIBLIOGRAPHIE SÉLECTIVE

0. La bibliographie présentée ici n'a d'autre but que d'orienter le lecteur intéressé dans le choix de lectures plus approfondies. La problématique du *mot* est très vaste, et a son origine dans l'ambiguïté du terme même, qui peut désigner une unité phonologique ou (ortho)graphique, ou un élément grammatical (morphosyntaxique). Dans l'usage lexicographique (qui s'est répandu dans les milieux didactiques), le mot désigne une entité définie à partir de considérations phonologiques, orthographiques et grammaticales (morphologiques et constructionnelles), mais dépouillée de certaines caractéristiques («accidents»), qui la font entrer dans des paradigmes flexionnels: le genre, le nombre, le cas, le temps, le mode, la voix, etc. C'est ainsi qu'on parlera à propos de la forme écrite <vers> en français de trois mots: *ver* (substantif masculin, au pluriel), *vers* (substantif masculin, singulier et pluriel), *vers* (mot invariable). De même, on parlera du «mot» *courir* en rapport avec les formes *(il) courait, (il) courra, (il a) couru,* etc. Sur l'ambiguïté du terme «mot», voir:

LYONS, J. 1968. *Introduction to theoretical linguistics.* Cambridge: University Press (p. 68-70; 196-206).

1. La définition du mot s'insère dans un contexte plus large: celui d'une caractérisation des *unités linguistiques*. Ce problème, qui relève de l'épistémologie de la linguistique et de la pratique descriptive est traité dans l'ouvrage de

EBELING, C.L. 1959. *Linguistic units* (Janua Linguarum, 12). 's Gravenhage: Mouton.

Quant à la définition du mot comme unité linguistique et son rapport avec d'autres unités, nous renvoyons aux travaux suivants, dont certains contiennent des bibliographies détaillées:

GRAFF, W.L. 1929. «The word and the sentence». *Language* 5. 163-188.
GREENBERG, J.H. 1957. *Essays in linguistics.* Chicago: The University of Chicago Press (chapitre II: «The definition of linguistic units»).
HIORTH, F. 1958. «On defining 'word'». *Studia Linguistica* 12. 1-26.

HOCKETT, Ch.F. 1958. *A course in modern linguistics*. New York: The Macmillan Company (p. 166-169).

KRÁMSKÝ, J. 1969. *The word as a linguistic unit* (Janua Linguarum, series minor, 75). The Hague-Paris: Mouton.

ROSETTI, A. 1947. *Le mot. Esquisse d'une théorie générale*. Deuxième édition revue et augmentée. Copenhague: E. Munksgaard; Bucureşti: Institutul de linguistică română.

SEILER, H. 1964. «On defining the word». *Proceedings of the ninth international congress of linguists, Cambridge, Mass. 1962*, 767-770. The Hague-Paris: Mouton.

SETÄLÄ, E. 1932. «Le mot». *Journal de la Société finno-ougrienne* 43. 17-34.

TOGEBY, K. 1949. «Qu'est-ce qu'un mot?». *Travaux du Cercle linguistique de Copenhague* 5. 97-111.

Ce dernier article contient d'importantes remarques sur la définition du mot en fonction des niveaux d'analyse linguistique.

2.0. Parmi les définitions du mot, il faut d'abord mentionner celles qui en font une unité substantielle, soit à un niveau très abstrait (association d'un sens à une forme; signe (minimal) dans la communication), soit à un niveau plus concret (forme libre ne faisant pas partie d'une autre forme libre). C'est à l'un de ces types qu'il faut rattacher les définitions du mot qu'on trouve chez:

BLOCH, B. - G.L. TRAGER. 1942. *Outline of linguistic analysis*. Baltimore: Waverly Press (p. 53-54).

BLOOMFIELD, L. 1926. «A set of postulates for the science of language». *Language* 2. 153-164 (p. 156).

BLOOMFIELD, L. 1933. *Language*. New York: Holt, Rinehart & Winston (p. 179).

GARDINER, A.H. 1932. *The theory of speech and language*. Oxford: Clarendon Press (p. 63, 88, 119-129).

LAZICZIUS, G. 1945. «La définition du mot». *Cahiers Ferdinand de Saussure* 5. 32-37 (= *Selected writings of Gyula Laziczius*, ed. by Th.A. Sebeok, 90-94. The Hague: Mouton, 1966).

MEILLET, A. 1921. *Linguistique historique et linguistique générale*. I. Paris: Champion (p. 30).

REICHLING, A. 1967². *Het woord. Een studie omtrent de grondslag van taal en taalgebruik*. Zwolle: Tjeenk Willink (1935¹).

SECHEHAYE, A. 1926. *Essai sur la structure logique de la phrase*. Paris: Champion (p. 14).

SEIDEL, E. 1947. «Wort und Satz». *Revue des études indo-européennes* 4. 50-64.

2.1. Le mot peut aussi être défini comme le résultat d'une procédure de segmentation appliquée par le linguiste. Cette vue, développée par

GARVIN, P.L. 1972². *On linguistic method. Selected papers* (Janua Linguarum, series minor, 30). The Hague-Paris: Mouton (p. 33-34; 1964¹: 32-33),

implique qu'une unité «mot» ne se laisse définir qu'en fonction de données linguistiques qui la justifient. Il faut donc prévoir que le mot n'est pas une unité pertinente dans toutes les langues. C'est d'ailleurs la conclusion de

MILEWSKI, T. 1951. «The conception of the word in the languages of North American natives». *Lingua Posnaniensis* 3. 248-268,

qui défend la thèse que certaines langues amérindiennes (langues Na-déné, athapascan, le maidu, le takelma et plusieurs dialectes du sioux) n'ont pas de «mots» (définis comme des unités morphosyntaxiques qu'on peut délimiter à l'intérieur d'une phrase).

2.2. L'impossibilité d'harmoniser une définition du mot comme unité substantielle avec des analyses de données concrètes a conduit certains linguistes à rejeter la notion de «mot» et à la remplacer éventuellement par une autre notion, plus opérante:

BALLY, Ch. 1932. *Linguistique générale et linguistique française*. Paris: Leroux (p. 288).

MARTINET, A. 1960. *Éléments de linguistique générale*. Paris: A. Colin (§4.15 à 4.17).

MARTINET, A. 1968. «Mot et synthème». *Lingua* 21. 294-302.

3. Le mot a souvent été défini à partir d'un fait établi: l'existence de *classes de mots*. Cela n'est pas seulement le cas dans les grammaires traditionnelles, mais également chez

BRØNDAL, V. 1943. *Essais de linguistique générale*. Copenhague: Munksgaard (p. 117-123: «La constitution du mot»).

Le système des parties du discours représente une tentative, ayant une longue tradition, de constituer des classes de mots, caractérisées par une unité morphologique, sémantique et syntaxique (valence; distribution). La justification du schéma «européen» des parties du discours, et son applicabilité (totale ou partielle) à des langues non indo-européennes ont fait l'objet de plusieurs études, dont nous retenons les suivantes:

HELBIG, G. 1968. «Zum Problem der Wortarten, Satzglieder und Formklassen». R. Růžička ed., *Probleme der strukturellen Grammatik und Semantik*, 55-85. Leipzig: Karl-Marx-Universität.

HERMANN, E. 1928. «Die Wortarten». *Nachrichten von der Gesellschaft der Wissenschaften zu Göttingen* 1928. 1-44.

KHLEBNIKOVA, I.B. 1963. «Funkcional'nye osnovy vydelenija klassov slov». *Problemy morfologičeskogo stroja germanskich jazykov*, 36-47. Moskva: Ak. Nauk.

Lingua 17 (1967): *Word Classes* (contributions de J. Carnochan, D. Crystal, F.J. Daniels, H. Hoijer, F. Householder, P. Kratochvíl, P. Matthews, S. Newman, F.R. Palmer, R.H. Robins, E.B. Van Wyk).

LYONS, J. 1966. «Towards a 'notional' theory of 'the parts of speech'». *Journal of Linguistics* 2. 209-236.

SANDMANN, M. 1940. «Substantiv, Adjektiv-Adverb und Verb als sprachliche Formen. Bemerkungen zur Theorie der Wortarten». *Indogermanische Forschungen* 57. 81-112.

SCHMID, W.P. 1972. *Skizze einer allgemeinen Theorie der Wortarten*. (Abhandlungen der Akademie der Wissenschaften und der Literatur zu Mainz, Geistes- und sozialwissenschaftliche Klasse 1970, 5). Wiesbaden: F. Steiner Verlag.

ORIENTALISTE, P.B. 41, B-3000 Leuven